LEARN GERMAN WITH BEGINNER STORIES

ISBN: 978-1-988830-07-0

D1475397

This book is published by Bermuda Word. It has been created with specialized software that produces a three line interlinear format.

Please contact us if you would like a pdf version of this book with different font, font size, or font colors and/or less words per page!

LEARN-TO-READ-FOREIGN-LANGUAGES.COM

Dear Reader and Language Learner!

You're reading the Paperback edition of Bermuda Word's interlinear and pop-up HypLern Reader App. Before you start reading German, please read this explanation of our method.

Since we want you to read German and to learn German, our method consists primarily of word-for-word literal translations, but we add idiomatic English if this helps understanding the sentence.

For example:
Er fing von neuem an zu schreien.
He caught from new on to scream
[He started again to scream.]

The HypLern method entails that you re-read the text until you know the high frequency words just by reading, and then mark and learn the low frequency words in your reader or practice them with our brilliant App.

Don't forget to take a look at the e-book App with integrated learning software that we offer at learn-to-read-foreign-languages.com! For more info check the last two pages of this e-book!

Thanks for your patience and enjoy the story and learning German!

Kees van den End

LEARN-TO-READ-FOREIGN-LANGUAGES.COM

INHALTSANGABE
CONTENTS

4   Die Rübe

DIE RÜBE
THE TURNIP

Es waren einmal zwei Brüder, die dienten beide als
It were once two brothers who served both as
(There)

Soldaten, und war der eine reich, der andere arm. Da
soldiers and was the one rich the other one poor Then

wollte der Arme sich aus seiner Not helfen, zog den
wanted the poor one himself out of his need help pulled the

Soldatenrock aus und ward ein Bauer. Also grub und
soldier's skirt off and became a farmer Thus dug and

hackte er sein Stückchen Acker und säte Rübsamen.
chopped he his bit of field and sowed turnip seed

Der Same ging auf, und es wuchs da eine Rübe,
The seed went up and it grew there a turnip

die ward groß und stark und zusehends dicker und
that became large and strong and visibly more thick and

wollte gar nicht aufhören zu wachsen, so daß sie
wanted indeed not stop to grow so that it

eine Fürstin aller Rüben heißen konnte:
a queen of all turnips called could be

denn	nimmer	war	so	eine	gesehen,	und	wird	auch
because	never	was	such	one	seen	and	would	also

nimmer	wieder	gesehen	werden.
never	again	seen	become

Zuletzt	war	sie	so	groß,	daß	sie	allein	einen	ganzen
Lastly	was	it	so	big	that	it	alone	one	whole

Wagen	anfüllte,	und	zwei	Ochsen	daran	ziehen	mußten,
cart	filled	and	two	oxen	it	pull	had

und	der	Bauer	wußte	nicht,	was	er	damit	anfangen
and	the	farmer	knew	not	what	he	with it	begin

sollte,	und	ob's	sein	Glück	oder	sein	Unglück	wäre.
should	and	if it	his	fortune	or	his	misfortune	were

Endlich	dachte	er	"verkaufst	du	sie,	was	wirst	du
Finally	thought	he	sell	you	it	what	will	you

Großes	dafür	bekommen,	und	willst	du	sie	selber
a lot	for it	get	and	want	you	them	self

essen,	so	tun	die	kleinen	Rüben	denselben	Dienst:
eat	so	do	the	small	turnips	the same	service

am	besten	ist,	du	bringst	sie	dem	König	und	machst
best		is	you	bring	it	to the	king	and	make

ihm	eine	Verehrung	damit."
him	an	honor	with it

7 Die Rübe

Also	lud	er	sie	auf	den	Wagen,	spannte	zwei	Ochsen
Thus	loaded	he	it	on	the	cart	harnessed	two	oxen

vor,	brachte	sie	an	den	Hof	und	schenkte	sie	dem
in front	brought	it	to	the	court	and	gave	it	the

König.	"Was	ist	das	für	ein	seltsam	Ding?"	sagte	der
king	What	is	that	for	a	strange	thing	said	the

König,	"mir	ist	viel	Wunderliches	vor	die	Augen
king	me	is (has)	much	wonderful things	before	the	eyes

gekommen,	aber	so	ein	Ungetüm	noch	nicht;	aus	was
come	but	such	a	monster	yet	not	from	what kind

für	Samen	mag	die	gewachsen	sein?	oder	dir	geräts
of	seed	may	that	grown	be	or	you	did it

allein	und	du	bist	ein	Glückskind."
alone	and	you	are	a	child of fortune

"Ach	nein,"	sagte	der	Bauer,	"ein	Glückskind	bin	ich
Oh	no	said	the	farmer	a	child of fortune	am	I

nicht,	ich	bin	ein	armer	Soldat,	der,	weil	er	sich
not	I	am	a	poor	soldier	who	because	he	himself

nicht	mehr	ernähren	konnte,	den	Soldatenrock	an	den
not	anymore	nourish	could	the	soldier's skirt (uniform)	on	a

Nagel	hing	und	das	Land	baute."
nail	hung	and	the	land	cultivated

8 Die Rübe

"Ich habe noch einen Bruder, der ist reich, und Euch,
I have still one brother who is rich and you

Herr König, auch wohl bekannt, ich aber, weil ich
lord king also well known I however because I

nichts habe, bin von aller Welt vergessen." Da
nothing have am of the whole world forsaken There

empfand der König Mitleid mit ihm und sprach, "Deiner
felt the king compassion with him and spoke Your

Armut sollst du überhoben und so von mir beschenkt
poverty will you lift high and so by me gifted

werden, daß du wohl deinem reichen Bruder gleich
become that you indeed your rich brother equal

kommst."
come

Da schenkte er ihm eine Menge Gold, Äcker, Wiesen
Then gave he him a quantity gold fields meadows

und Herden und machte ihn steinreich, so daß des
and herds and made him stone-rich so that the
(very rich)

andern Bruders Reichtum gar nicht konnte damit
other brother's wealth hardly not could with it

verglichen werden.
compared become

9 Die Rübe

Als	dieser	hörte,	was	sein	Bruder	mit	einer	einzigen
As	this	heard	what	his	brother	with	a	single

Rübe	erworben	hatte,	beneidete	er	ihn	und	sann	hin
turnip	acquired	had	envied	he	him	and	contemplated	here

und	her,	wie	er	sich	auch	ein	solches	Glück
and	there	how	he	himself	also	a	such (similar)	fortune

zuwenden	könnte.
beget	could

Er	wollt's	aber	noch	viel	gescheiter	anfangen,	nahm
He	wanted it	however	even	more	more clever	begin	took

Gold	und	Pferde	und	brachte	sie	dem	König	und
gold	and	horses	and	brought	them	the	king	and

meinte	nicht	anders,	der	würde	ihm	ein	viel	größeres
thought	nothing	else	he	would	him	a	much	larger

Gegengeschenk	machen:
counter gift	make

denn	hätte	sein	Bruder	so	viel	für	eine	Rübe
because	had	his	brother	so	much	for	one	turnip

bekommen,	was	würde	es	ihm	für	so	schöne	Dinge
gotten	what	became	it	him	for	so	beautiful	things

nicht	alles	tragen.
not	all	carry

10 Die Rübe

Der König nahm das Geschenk und sagte, er wüßte
The king took the gift and said he would know

ihm nichts wiederzugeben, das seltener und besser wäre
him nothing to give back that more rare and better would be

als die große Rübe. Also mußte der Reiche seines
as the large turnip Thus had the rich one his

Bruders Rübe auf einen Wagen legen und nach Haus
brother's turnip on a cart put and to house

fahren lassen. Daheim wußte er nicht, an wem er
drive let At home knew he not on who he

seinen Zorn und Ärger auslassen sollte, bis ihm böse
his anger and annoyance vent should until to him bad

Gedanken kamen und er beschloß, seinen Bruder zu
thoughts came and he decided his brother to

töten.
kill

Er gewann Mörder, die mußten sich in einen Hinterhalt
He acquired murderers who had themselves in an ambush
(hired)

stellen, und darauf ging er zu seinem Bruder und
place and thereupon went he to his brother and

sprach:
said

"Lieber Bruder, ich weiß einen heimlichen Schatz, den
Dear brother I know a secret treasure that

wollen wir miteinander heben und teilen."
shall we with one another lift out and share

Der andere ließ sich's auch gefallen und ging ohne
The other one let himself it also please and went without

Arg mit. Als sie aber hinauskamen, stürzten die Mörder
suspicion (with) As they however came out fell the murderers

über ihn her, banden ihn und wollten ihn an einen
over him (to) bound him and wanted him on a
(from)

Baum hängen. Indem sie eben darüber waren, erscholl
tree hang In that they just about it were sounded
(When)

aus der Ferne lauter Gesang und Hufschlag, daß ihnen
from the distance loud singing and hoof impact so that them
(the sound of hooves)

der Schrecken in den Leib fuhr und sie
the fright in the body drove and they

über Hals und Kopf ihren Gefangenen in den Sack
over neck and head their prisoner in the bag
(very quickly)

steckten, am Ast hinaufwanden und die Flucht ergriffen.
put onto the branch pulled up and the escape seized
(started)

13   Die Rübe

Er aber arbeitete oben, bis er ein Loch im Sack
He however worked above until he a hole in the bag

hatte, wodurch er den Kopf stecken konnte.
had through which he the head put could

Wer aber des Wegs kam, war nichts als ein
Who however by the road came was nothing as a

fahrender Schüler, ein junger Geselle, der fröhlich sein
traveling student a young fellow who merrily his

Lied singend durch den Wald auf der Straße daherritt.
song singing through the forest up the road rode along

Wie der oben nun merkte, daß einer unter ihm
As the one above now noticed that one under him

vorbeiging, rief er, "Sei mir gegrüßt zu guter Stunde."
passed called he Be by me greeted on this good moment

Der Schüler guckte sich überall um, wußte nicht, wo
The student looked himself everywhere around knew not where

die Stimme herschallte, endlich sprach er, "Wer ruft
the voice sounded from finally spoke he Who calls

mir?"
me

14　Die Rübe

Da antwortete er aus dem Wipfel:
Then answered he from the treetop

"Erhebe deine Augen, ich sitze hier oben im Sack;
Raise your eyes I sit here above in the bag

der Weisheit: in kurzer Zeit habe ich große Dinge
of wisdom in brief time have I great things
(the)

gelernt, dagegen sind alle Schulen ein Wind: um ein
learned compared to that are all schools a wind in a

weniges, so werde ich ausgelernt haben, herabsteigen
while so will I finished learning have climb down

und weiser sein als alle Menschen."
and more wise be as all humans

"Ich verstehe die Gestirne und Himmelszeichen, das
I understand the stars and sky signs the

Wehen aller Winde, den Sand im Meer, Heilung der
blowing of all winds the sand in the sea Healing of the

Krankheit, die Kräfte der Kräuter, Vögel und Steine."
illnesses the powers of the herbs birds and stones

15 Die Rübe

16 Die Rübe

"Wärst du einmal darin, du würdest fühlen, was für
Would be you once in there you would feel what kind of

Herrlichkeit aus dem Sack der Weisheit fließt."
glory out of the bag of wisdom flows
(the)

Der Schüler, wie er das alles hörte, erstaunte und
The student as he that all heard (was) surprised and

sprach, "Gesegnet sei die Stunde, wo ich dich
spoke Blessed is the hour where I you

gefunden habe, könnt ich nicht auch ein wenig in den
found have can I not also a little in the

Sack kommen?"
bag come

Oben der antwortete, als tät er's nicht gerne, "Eine
Above the one answered as did he it not gladly A

kleine Weile will ich dich wohl hineinlassen für Lohn
small while will I you well let in for wages

und gute Worte, aber du mußt doch noch eine
and good words but you must however still one

Stunde warten, es ist ein Stück übrig, das ich erst
hour wait it is a part remaining that I first
(there)

lernen muß."
learn must

17 Die Rübe

Als der Schüler ein wenig gewartet hatte, war ihm die
As the student a little waited had was to him the

Zeit zu lang und er bat, daß er doch möchte
time too long and he asked that he yet would like

hineingelassen werden, sein Durst nach Weisheit wäre
let in become his thirst for wisdom were

gar zu groß. Da stellte sich der oben, als gäbe er
indeed too great There, Then acted himself the one above as if gave he

endlich nach, und sprach, "Damit ich aus dem Haus
finally in and spoke So that I of the house

der Weisheit heraus kann, mußt du den Sack am
of wisdom out can must you the bag by the
(the)

Strick herunterlassen, so sollst du eingehen." Also ließ
rope lower so shall you enter Thus let

der Schüler ihn herunter, band den Sack auf und
the student him down bound the bag open and

befreite ihn, dann rief er selber, "Nun zieh mich recht
released him then called he self Now pull me really

geschwind hinauf," und wollt geradstehend in den Sack
quickly up and wanted at that moment in the bag

einschreiten.
enter

"Halt!", sagte der andere, "so gehts nicht an," packte
Stop said the other one so not on took
(well)

ihn beim Kopf, steckte ihn umgekehrt in den Sack,
him by the head put him turned around in the bag

schnürte zu und zog den Jünger der Weisheit am
tied fast and pulled the disciple of wisdom by the
(the)

Strick baumwärts, dann schwengelte er ihn in der Luft
rope treewards then moved he him in the air

und sprach "wie steht's, mein lieber Geselle? siehe,
and said how stands it my dear fellow see

schon fühlst du, daß dir die Weisheit kommt, und
already feel you that to you the wisdom comes and

machst gute Erfahrung, sitze also fein ruhig, bis du
make good experience sit thus fine calm until you
(get)

klüger wirst."
more intelligent become

Damit stieg er auf des Schülers Pferd, ritt fort,
Thus rose he on the student's horse rode away

schickte aber nach einer Stunde jemand, der ihn
sent however after one hour someone that him

wieder herablassen mußte.
again let down had to

19　Die Rübe

DIE BREMER STADTMUSIKANTEN
THE BREMEN CITY MUSICIANS

Es	war	einmal	ein	Mann,	der	hatte	einen	Esel,
It (There)	was	once	a	man	who	had	a	donkey

welcher	schon	lange	Jahre	unverdrossen	die	Säcke	in
which	already	long	years	undauntedly	the	bags	in

die	Mühle	getragen	hatte.	Nun	aber	gingen	die	Kräfte
the	mill	carried	had	Now	however	went	the	forces

des	Esels	zu	Ende,	so	daß	er	zur	Arbeit	nicht	mehr
of the	donkey	to (their)	end	so	that	he	for the	work	not	(any)more

taugte.	Da	dachte	der	Herr	daran,	ihn	wegzugehen.
was suited	Then	thought	the	master	of it	him	to leave

Aber	der	Esel	merkte,	daß	sein	Herr	etwas	Böses	im
But	the	donkey	noticed	that	his	master	something	bad	in

Sinn	hatte,	lief	fort	und	machte	sich	auf	den	Weg
mind	had	ran	away	and	made (got)	himself	on	the	road

nach	Bremen.	Dort,	so	meinte	er,	könnte	er	ja
to	Bremen	There	so	believed	he	could	he	well

Stadtmusikant	werden.
city musician	become

23 Die Bremer Stadtmusikanten

Als er schon eine Weile gegangen war, fand er einen
As he already a while gone was, found he one

Jagdhund am Wege liegen, der jämmerlich heulte.
hunting dog on the road laying who deplorably howled

"Warum heulst du denn so, Packan?" fragte der Esel.
Why howl you then so Holdfast asked the donkey

"Ach", sagte der Hund, "weil ich alt bin, jeden Tag
Oh said the dog because I old am every day

schwächer werde und auch nicht mehr auf die Jagd
more weak become and also not anymore on the hunt

kann, wollte mich mein Herr totschießen. Da hab ich
can wanted me my lord shoot dead There have I

Reißaus genommen. Aber womit soll ich nun mein Brot
taken off But with what should I now my bread

verdienen?"
earn

"Weißt du, was", sprach der Esel, "ich gehe nach
Know you what spoke the donkey I go to

Bremen und werde dort Stadtmusikant."
Bremen and will become there city musician

25 Die Bremer Stadtmusikanten

"Komm mit mir und laß dich auch bei der Musik
Come with me and let yourself also by the music

annehmen. Ich spiele die Laute, und du schlägst die
to take in I play the lute and you strike the

Pauken." Der Hund war einverstanden, und sie gingen
bass drums The dog was in agreement and they went

mitsammen weiter.
together further

Es dauerte nicht lange, da sahen sie eine Katze am
It lasted not long then saw they a cat on the
(when)

Wege sitzen, die machte ein Gesicht wie drei Tage
road sit that made a face like three days

Regenwetter. "Was ist denn dir in die Quere
rainy weather What is then you in the crossing
(way)

gekommen, alter Bartputzer?" fragte der Esel.
come old Whiskergroomer asked the donkey

"Wer kann da lustig sein, wenn's einem an den
Who can then happy be if it one on the
[the life is in

Kragen geht", antwortete die Katze.
collar goes answered the cat
danger]

27 Die Bremer Stadtmusikanten

"Weil ich nun alt bin, meine Zähne stumpf werden
Because I now old are my teeth blunt become

und ich lieber hinter dem Ofen sitze und spinne, als
and I rather behind the furnace sit and purr than

nach Mäusen herumjage, hat mich meine Frau ersäufen
after mice chase around has me my lady drown

wollen. Ich konnte mich zwar noch davonschleichen,
want I could myself just still sneak away

aber nun ist guter Rat teuer. Wo soll ich jetzt hin?"
but now is good advice expensive Where must I now (go) to

"Geh mit uns nach Bremen! Du verstehst dich doch
Go with us to Bremen You understand yourself indeed
(are familiar with)

auf die Nachtmusik, da kannst du Stadtmusikant
(on) the night music then can you city musician

werden."
become

Die Katze hielt das für gut und ging mit.
The cat held that for well and went with
(together)

Als	die	drei	so	miteinander	gingen,	kamen	sie	an
As	the	three	so	with one another	went	came	they	by

einem	Hof	vorbei.	Da	saß	der	Haushahn	auf	dem	Tor
a	yard	along	There	sat	the	house cock	on	the	gate

und	schrie	aus	Leibeskräften.
and	cried	out of	body forces (all his might)

"Du	schreist	einem	durch	Mark	und	Bein",	sprach	der
You	cry	one	through [heart-rending	marrow	and	bone]	spoke	the

Esel,	"was	hast	du	vor?"
Donkey	what	have [do you	you	for mean]

"Die	Hausfrau	hat	der	Köchin	befohlen,	mir	heute	abend
The	housewife	had	the	cook	ordered	me	today evening (tonight)	

den	Kopf	abzusschlagen.	Morgen,	am	Sonntag,	haben
the	head	off to chop	Tomorrow	on	sunday	have

sie	Gäste,	da	wollen	sie	mich	in	der	Suppe	essen.
they	guests	then	want	they	me	in	the	soup	eat

Nun	schrei	ich	aus	vollem	Hals,	solang	ich	noch	kann."
Now	cry	I	out of	full neck (all might)		solang	I	still	can

"Ei was" sagte der Esel, "zieh lieber mit uns fort, wir
Well what said the donkey leave rather with us (away) we

gehen nach Bremen, etwas Besseres als den Tod
go to Bremen something better than death

findest du überall. Du hast eine gute Stimme, und
find you everywhere You have a good voice and

wenn wir mitsammen musizieren, wird es gar herrlich
if we together make music becomes it really wonderful

klingen." Dem Hahn gefiel der Vorschlag, und sie
sound The cock pleased the suggestion and they

gingen alle vier mitsammen fort. Sie konnten aber die
went all four together away They could however the
(on the road)

Stadt Bremen an einem Tag nicht erreichen und kamen
city Bremen in one day not reach and came

abends in einen Wald, wo sie übernachten wollten. Der
in the evening in a forest where they stay overnight wanted The

Esel und der Hund legten sich unter einen großen
donkey and the dog put themselves under a large

Baum, die Katze kletterte auf einen Ast, und der
tree the cat climbed on a branch and the

Hahn flog bis in den Wipfel, wo es am sichersten
cock flew up in the treetop where it (to the) safest

für ihn war.
for him was

31 Die Bremer Stadtmusikanten

Ehe er einschlief, sah er sich noch einmal nach allen
Before *he* *fell asleep* *saw* *he* *himself* *still* *once* *to* *all*

vier Windrichtungen um. Da bemerkte er einen
four *wind directions* *around* *There* *noticed* *he* *a*

Lichtschein. Er sagte seinen Gefährten, daß in der
light shine *He* *said* *his* *companions* *that* *in* *the*

Nähe ein Haus sein müsse, denn er sehe ein Licht.
proximity *a* *house* *be* *must* *because* *he* *saw* *a* *light*

Der Esel antwortete: "So wollen wir uns aufmachen
The *donkey* *answered* *So (then)* *will* *we* *ourselves* *get up*

und noch hingehen, denn hier ist die Herberge
and *still* *go there* *because* *here* *is* *the* *lodging*

schlecht." Der Hund meinte, ein paar Knochen und
bad *The* *dog* *thought* *a* *few* *bones* *and*

etwas Fleisch daran täten ihm auch gut.
some *meat* *to it* *would do* *him* *also* *well*

Also machten sie sich auf den Weg nach der
Thus *made* *they* *themselves* *up* *the* *road* *to* *the*

Gegend, wo das Licht war.
area *where* *the* *light* *was*

33 Die Bremer Stadtmusikanten

Bald sahen sie es heller schimmern, und es wurde
Soon saw they it more brightly gleam and it became

immer größer, bis sie vor ein hellerleuchtetes
always larger until they before a bright shining

Räuberhaus kamen.
robbers' house came
(thieves den)

Der Esel, als der größte, näherte sich dem Fenster
The donkey as the largest approached himself to the window

und schaute hinein.
and looked inside

"Was siehst du, Grauschimmel?" fragte der Hahn.
What see you Gray asked the cock

"Was ich sehe?" antwortete der Esel. "Einen gedeckten
What I see answered the donkey A covered

Tisch mit schönem Essen und Trinken, und Räuber
table with beautiful food and drinks and robbers

sitzen rundherum und lassen sich's gutgehen!"
sit around and let themselves go well

"Das wäre etwas für uns", sprach der Hahn.
That would be something for us spoke the cock

Da überlegten die Tiere, wie sie es anfangen könnten,
Then deliberated the animals how they it begin could

die Räuber hinauszujagen.
the robbers to hunt out

Endlich fanden sie ein Mittel. Der Esel stellte sich mit
Finally found they a means The donkey placed himself with
(way)

den Vorderfüßen auf das Fenster, der Hund sprang auf
the front feet up on the window the dog jumped up on
(hooves)

des Esels Rücken, die Katze kletterte auf den Hund,
the donkey's back the cat climbed on the Dog

und zuletzt flog der Hahn hinauf und setzte sich der
and last flew the cock up and set himself the

Katze auf den Kopf. Als das geschehen war, fingen
cat up on the head As that happened was caught

sie auf ein Zeichen an, ihre Musik zu machen:
they at a sign with their music to make

der Esel schrie, der Hund bellte, die Katze miaute,
the donkey cried the dog barked the cat mewed

und der Hahn krähte. Darauf stürzten sie durch das
and the cock crowed Whereupon fell they through the

Fenster in die Stube hinein, daß die Scheiben klirrten.
window in the room inside so that the plates rattled

Die Räuber fuhren bei dem entsetzlichen Geschrei in
The robbers went at the terrible shouting in
(jumped)

die Höhe. Sie meinten, ein Gespenst käme herein, und
the air They thought a ghost had come in and

flohen in größter Furcht in den Wald hinaus.
fled in great fear into the forest outside

Nun setzten sie die vier Gesellen an den Tisch, und
Now set they the four friends at the table and

jeder aß nach Herzenslust von den Speisen, die ihm
everyone ate to heart's desire of the food that to him

am besten schmeckten.
to the best tasted

37 Die Bremer Stadtmusikanten

Als	sie	fertig	waren,	löschten	sie	das	Licht	aus,	und
As	they	finished	were	turned	they	the	light	off	and

jeder	suchte	sich	eine	Schlafstätte	nach	seinem
everyone	searched	himself	a	place to sleep	after	his

Geschmack.	Der	Esel	legte	sich	auf	den	Mist,	der
taste	The	donkey	put	himself	up	the	dung	the

Hund	hinter	die	Tür,	die	Katze	auf	den	Herd	bei	der
dog	behind	the	door	the	cat	up on	the	stove	by	the

warmen	Asche,	und	der	Hahn	flog	auf	das	Dach
warm	ashes	and	the	cock	flew	on	the	roof

hinauf.	Und	weil	sie	müde	waren	von	ihrem	langen
up	And	since	they	tired	were	of	their	long

Weg,	schliefen	sie	bald	ein.
road (voyage)	slept	they	soon	(in)

Als	Mitternacht	vorbei	war	und	die	Räuber	von	weitem
As	midnight	past	was	and	the	robbers	from	afar

sahen,	daß	kein	Licht	mehr	im	Haus	brannte	und
saw	that	no	light	anymore	in the	house	burned	and

alles	ruhig	schien,	sprach	der	Hauptmann:
everything	calm	seemed	spoke	the	chief

"Wir hätten uns doch nicht sollen ins Bockshorn jagen
We have ourselves indeed not should in the goat's horn chase (to frighten)

lassen." Er schickte einen Räuber zurück, um
let He sent one robber back over

nachzusehen, ob noch jemand im Hause wäre.
to check whether still someone in the house was

Der Räuber fand alles still. Er ging in die Küche
The robber found everything quiet He went into the kitchen

und wollte ein Licht anzünden. Da sah er die feurigen
and wanted a light turn on There saw he the fiery

Augen der Katze und meinte, es wären glühende
eyes of the cat and thought it were glowing

Kohlen. Er hielt ein Schwefelhölzchen daran, daß es
coals He held a sulphur-little wood to it so that it
(match)

Feuer fangen sollte. Aber die Katze verstand keinen
fire catch would But the cat understood no
(thought it)

Spaß, sprang ihm ins Gesicht und kratzte ihn
fun jumped him in the face and scratched him

aus Leibeskräften. Da erschrak er gewaltig und wollte
off body forces Then frightened he enormously and wanted
(out of all might)

zur Hintertür hinauslaufen.
to the back door run out

Aber der Hund, der da lag, sprang auf und biß ihn
But the dog who there laid jumped up and bit him

ins Bein. Als der Räuber über den Hof am Misthaufen
in the leg As the robber over the yard along the dung heap

vorbeirannte, gab ihm der Esel noch einen tüchtigen
ran by gave him the donkey still an sound

Schlag mit dem Hinterfuß. Der Hahn aber, der von
kick with the hind feet The cock however who by
(hooves)

dem Lärm aus dem Schlaf geweckt worden war, rief
the noise out of the sleep waked become was called

vom Dache herunter: "Kikeriki!"
from the roof down Kikeriki

Da lief der Räuber, was er konnte, zu seinem
There ran the robber what he could to his

Hauptmann zurück und sprach: "Ach, in dem Haus sitzt
chief back and spoke Oh in the house sits

eine greuliche Hexe, die hat mich angehaucht und mir
a horrible witch she has me blew at and me

mit ihren langen Fingern das Gesicht zerkratzt."
with her long fingers the face scratched

"An der Tür steht ein Mann mit einem Messer, der
By the door stands a man with a knife who

hat mich ins Bein gestochen. Auf dem Hof liegt ein
has me in the leg stabbed In the yard lies a

schwarzes Ungetüm, das hat mit einem Holzprügel auf
black monster that has with one wood stick at

mich losgeschlagen. Und oben auf dem Dache, da sitzt
me struck away And above on the roof there sits

der Richter, der rief: 'Bringt mir den Schelm her!' Da
the judge who called Brings me the rascal here Then

machte ich, daß ich fortkam."
made I that I came away

Von nun an getrauten sich die Räuber nicht mehr in
From now on trusted themselves the robbers not anymore in
            (dared)

das Haus. Den vier Bremer Stadtmusikanten aber
the house The four Bremen city musicians however

gefiel's darin so gut, daß sie nicht wieder hinaus
pleased it there so well that they not again out

wollten.
wanted

43   Die Bremer Stadtmusikanten

DAUMESDICK
THUMBTHICK

Es war ein armer Bauersmann, der saß abends beim
It was a poor farmer that sat in the evening by the
(There)

Herd und schürte das Feuer, und die Frau saß und
stove and poked the fire and the woman sat and

spann. Da sprach er "wie ist's so traurig, daß wir
spun Then spoke he how is it so sad that we

keine Kinder haben! es ist so still bei uns, und in
no children have it is so quiet with us and in

den andern Häusern ist's so laut und lustig."
the other houses is it so noisy and merry

"Ja," antwortete die Frau und seufzte, "wenn's nur ein
Yes answered the woman and sighed if it only a

einziges wäre, und wenn's auch ganz klein wäre, nur
one would be and if it also completely small would be only

Daumens groß, so wollte ich schon zufrieden sein; wir
thumb large so would I already content be we

hätten's doch von Herzen lieb."
would have it nonetheless from the heart dear

47 Daumesdick

Nun	geschah	es,	daß	die	Frau	kränklich	ward	und
Now	happened	it	that	the	woman	in a condition (pregnant)	became	and

nach	sieben	Monaten	ein	Kind	gebar,	das	zwar	an
after	seven	months	a	child	bore	that	although	on

allen	Gliedern	vollkommen,	aber	nicht	länger	als	ein
all	members, bodyparts	perfect	but	not	longer	than	a

Daumen	war.	Da	sprachen	sie;	"es	ist,	wie	wir	es
thumb	was	There	spoke	they	it	is	as	we	it

gewünscht	haben,	und	es	soll	unser	liebes	Kind	sein,"
wished	have	and	it	shall	our	dear	child	be

und	nannten	es	nach	seiner	Gestalt	Daumesdick.	Sie
and	called	it	after	its	shape	Daumesdick (Thumbthick)	They

ließen's	nicht	an	Nahrung	fehlen,	aber	das	Kind	ward
let it	not	of	food	lack	but	the	child	became

nicht	größer,	sondern	blieb,	wie	es	in	der	ersten
not	larger	but	remained	as	it	in	the	first

Stunde	gewesen	war;	doch	schaute	es	verständig	aus
hour	been	was (had)	but	looked	it	sensible	through

den	Augen	und	zeigte	sich	bald	als	ein	kluges	und
the	eyes	and	showed	itself	soon	as	an	intelligent	and

behendes	Ding,	dem	alles	glückte,	was	es	anfing.
swift	thing	that (who)	everything	succeeded	which	it	began

Der Bauer machte sich eines Tages fertig, in den
The farmer made himself one day ready in the

Wald zu gehen und Holz zu fällen, da sprach er so
forest to go and wood to fell there, so spoke he so
(chop down)

vor sich hin; "nun wollt ich, daß einer da wäre, der
for himself out now would I that one there would be who

mir den Wagen nachbrächte."
for me the cart would after-bring

"O Vater," rief Daumesdick, "den Wagen will ich schon
O father called Daumesdick the cart will I well
(Thumbthick)

bringen, verlaßt Euch drauf, er soll zur bestimmten Zeit
bring trust you on it it shall at the determined time

im Walde sein."
in the forest be

Da lachte der Mann und sprach; "wie sollte das
There laughed the man and spoke how should that

zugehen, du bist viel zu klein, um das Pferd mit
happen you are much too small for to the horse with

dem Zügel zu leiten."
the reins to lead

"Das tut nichts, Vater, wenn nur die Mutter anspannen
That does nothing father if only (the) mother harness
(is not a problem)

will, ich setze mich dem Pferd ins Ohr und rufe ihm
will I set me the horse in ear and call it

zu, wie es gehen soll."
to how it go should

"Nun," antwortete der Vater, "einmal wollen wir's
Now answered the father once will we it

versuchen."
try

Als die Stunde kam, spannte die Mutter an und
As the hour came harnessed the mother (on) and

setzte Daumesdick ins Ohr des Pferdes, und dann rief
set Daumesdick in the ear of the horse and then called
(Thumbthick)

der Kleine, wie das Pferd gehen sollte, "jüh und joh!
the small one how the horse go should giddyup and giddyup

hott und har!" Da ging es ganz ordentlich als wie
go and shoo There went it completely proper as if

bei einem Meister, und der Wagen fuhr den rechten
by a master and the cart drove the correct

Weg nach dem Walde.
road to the forest

51 Daumesdick

Es	trug sich	zu,	als	er	eben	um	eine	Ecke	bog	und
It	carried itself to (happened)		as	it	just	around	a	corner	turned	and

der	Kleine;	"har,	har!"	rief,	daß	zwei	fremde	Männer
the	small one	shoo	shoo	called	that	two	unknown	men

daherkamen.
came along

"Mein,"	sprach	der	eine,	"was	ist	das?	da	fährt	ein
My	spoke	the	one	what	is	that	there	drives	a

Wagen,	und	ein	Fuhrmann	ruft	dem	Pferde	zu,	und
cart	and	a	wagoner	calls	the	horses	(to)	and

ist	doch	nicht	zu	sehen."
is	however	not	to	see

"Das	geht	nicht	mit	rechten	Dingen	zu,"	sagte	der
That	goes	not	with	right	things	on	said	the

andere,	"wir	wollen	dem	Karren	folgen	und	sehen,	wo
other one	we	want	the	cart	follow	and	see	where

er	anhält."
it	stops

Der	Wagen	aber	fuhr	vollends	in	den	Wald	hinein	und
The	cart	however	drove	completely	in	the	forest	inside	and

richtig	zu	dem	Platze,	wo	das	Holz	gehauen	ward.
correctly	to	the	place	where	the	wood	chopped	became (was being)

52 Daumesdick

Als Daumesdick seinen Vater erblickte, rief er ihm zu;
As Daumesdick (Thumbthick) his father saw called he him (to)

"siehst du, Vater, da bin ich mit dem Wagen, nun
see you father there am I with the Car now

hol mich runter."
get me down

Der Vater faßte das Pferd mit der Linken und holte
The father seized the Horse with the left and got

mit der Rechten sein Söhnlein aus dem Ohr, das sich
with the right one his little son out of the ear that (who) himself

ganz lustig auf einen Strohhalm niedersetzte.
very merry up on a straw set down

Als die beiden fremden Männer den Daumesdick
As the both strange men (strangers (the) Daumesdick (Thumbthick)

erblickten, wußten sie nicht, was sie vor Verwunderung
saw knew they not what they out of surprise

sagen sollten.
say should

53 Daumesdick

Da	nahm	der	eine	den	andern	beiseit	und	sprach:
There	took	the	one	the	other one	apart	and	spoke

"hör,	der	kleine	Kerl	könnte	unser	Glück	machen,	wenn
hear	the	small	chap	could	us	fortune	make	if

wir	ihn	in	einer	großen	Stadt	für	Geld	sehen	ließen,
we	it	in	a	large	city	for	money	see	let

wir	wollen	ihn	kaufen."
we	want	it	to buy

Sie	gingen	zu	den	Bauer	und	sprachen:
They	went	to	the	farmer	and	spoke

"verkauft	uns	den	kleinen	Mann,	er	soll's	gut	bei	uns
sell	us	the	small	man	he	will it	good	with	us

haben."
have

"Nein,"	antwortete	der	Vater,	"es	ist	mein	Herzblatt,	und
No	answered	the	father	it	is	my	heart leaf (apple of one's eye)	and

ist	mir	für	alles	Gold	in	der	Welt	nicht	feil!"
is	me	for	all the	gold	in	the	world	not	for sale

Daumesdick aber, als er von dem Handel gehört, war
Daumesdick however as he of the trade heard was
(Thumbthick)

an den Rockfalten seines Vaters hinaufgekrochen, stellte
on the skirt folds of his father crept up placed

sich ihm auf die Schulter und wisperte ihm ins Ohr;
himself him on the shoulder and whispered him in the ear

"Vater, gib mich nur hin, ich will schon wieder
Father give me just to I will (already) again

zurückkommen."
return

Da gab ihn der Vater für ein schönes Stück Geld
There gave him the father for a beautiful piece money

den beiden Männern hin. "Wo willst du sitzen?" ,
the both men to Where want you sit

sprachen sie zu ihm.
spoke they to him

"Ach, setzt mich nur auf den Rand von eurem Hut,
Oh set me just up the edge of your hat

da kann ich auf und ab spazieren und die Gegend
there can I up and down walk and the surroundings

betrachten, und falle doch nicht herunter."
regard and fall however not down

55 Daumesdick

Sie taten ihm den Willen, und als Daumesdick
They did for him the will and as Daumesdick (Thumbthick)

Abschied von seinem Vater genommen hatte, machten
leave of his father taken had made

sie sich mit ihm fort. So gingen sie, bis es dämmrig
they themselves with him away So went they until it dusky

ward, da sprach der Kleine; "hebt mich einmal
became then spoke the small one lift me once

herunter, es ist nötig."
down it is necessary

"Bleib nur droben," sprach der Mann, auf dessen Kopf
Remain just up there spoke the man on whose head

er saß, "ich will mir nichts draus machen, die Vögel
he sat I shall me nothing of it make The birds

lassen mir auch manchmal was drauf fallen."
let me also sometimes something on it fall

"Nein," sprach Daumesdick, "ich weiß auch, was sich
No spoke Daumesdick (Thumbthick) I know also what itself

schickt, hebt mich nur geschwind herab."
fits lift me just quickly down
(is decent)

57 Daumesdick

Der — The
Mann — man
nahm — took
den — the
Hut — hat
ab — off
und — and
setzte — set
den — the
Kleinen — small one

auf — on
einen — a
Acker — field
am — by the
Weg, — road
da — there
sprang — jumped
und — and
kroch — crept
er — he

ein — a
wenig — little
zwischen — between
den — the
Schollen — clods of earth
hin — here
und — and
her, — fro
dann — then

schlüpfte — slipped
er — he
plötzlich — suddenly
in — in
ein — a
Mausloch, — mouse hole
das — that
er — he
sich — himself

ausgesucht — found
hatte. — had
"Guten — Good
Abend, — evening
ihr — you
Herren, — gentlemen
geht — go
nur — just

ohne — without
mich — me
heim," — home
rief — called
er — he
ihnen — them
zu, — to
und — and
lachte — laughed
sie — them

aus. — (off)
Sie — They
liefen — ran
herbei — near
und — and
stachen — stung
mit — with
Stöcken — sticks
in — in
das — the

Mausloch, — mouse hole
aber — but
das — it
war — was
vergebliche — useless [futile
Mühe, — trouble]
Daumesdick — Daumesdick (Thumbthick)

kroch — crept
immer — always
weiter — further
zurück, — back
und — and
da — because
es — it
bald — soon
ganz — completely

dunkel — dark
ward, — became
so — so
mußten — had
sie — they
mit — with
Ärger — annoyance
und — and
mit — with
leerem — empty

Beutel — pouch (purse)
wieder — again
heim — home
wandern. — move

Als Daumesdick merkte, daß sie fort waren, kroch er
As　Daumesdick　noticed　that　they　away　were　crept　he
　　(Thumbthick)

aus dem unterirdischen Gang wieder hervor.
out of　the　underground　tunnel　again　out

"Es ist auf dem Acker in der Finsternis so gefährlich
It　is　on　the　field　in　the　darkness　so　dangerous

gehen," sprach er, "wie leicht bricht einer Hals und
to go　spoke　he　how　easily　breaks　one　neck　and

Bein."
leg

Zum Glück stieß er an ein leeres Schneckenhaus.
Fortunately　bumped　he　into　an　empty　snail's shell

"Gottlob," sagte er, "da kann ich die Nacht sicher
God praise　said　he　there　can　I　the　night　surely

zubringen," und setzte sich hinein.
bring through　and　set　himself　inside
(spend)

Nicht	lang,	als	er	eben	einschlafen	wollte,	so	hörte	er
Not	long	as	he	just	fall asleep	wanted	so	heard	he

zwei	Männer	vorübergehen,	davon	sprach	der	eine	"wie
two	men	pass	of them	spoke	the	one	how

wir's	nur	anfangen,	um	dem	reichen	Pfarrer	sein	Geld
we it	only	begin (can master)	to	the	rich	minister (religious profession)	his	money

und	sein	Silber	zu	holen?"
and	his	silver	to	get

"Das	könnt	ich	dir	sagen,"	rief	Daumesdick	dazwischen.
That	can	I	you	tell	called	Daumesdick (Thumbthick)	between them

"Was	war	das?"	sprach	der	eine	Dieb	erschrocken,	"ich
What	was	that	said	the	one	Thief	frightened	I

hörte	jemand	sprechen."	Sie	blieben	stehen	und
heard	someone	speak	They	remained standing (stopped)		and

horchten,	da	sprach	Daumesdick	wieder;	"nehmt	mich
listened carefully	there	spoke	Daumesdick (Thumbthick)	again	take	me

mit,	so	will	ich	euch	helfen."
with (you)	so	shall	I	you	help

"Wo bist du denn?"
Who are you then

"Sucht nur auf der Erde und merkt, wo die Stimme
Search only on the earth and notice where the voice
(look) (ground) (see)
herkommt," antwortete er.
comes from answered he

Da fanden ihn endlich die Diebe und hoben ihn in
There found him finally the thieves and lifted him in

die Höhe.
the height

"Du kleiner Wicht, was willst du uns helfen!" sprachen
You little gnome what want you us help said
(how)
sie.
they

"Seht," antwortete er, "ich krieche zwischen den
See answered he I creep between the

Eisenstäben in die Kammer des Pfarrers und reiche
iron bars in the room of the minister and reach
(religious functionary)

euch heraus, was ihr haben wollt."
you out what you have want

61 Daumesdick

"Wohlan,"   sagten   sie,   "wir   wollen   sehen,   was   du
Well   said   they   we   will   see   what   you

kannst."
can

Als   sie   bei   dem   Pfarrhaus   kamen,   kroch   Daumesdick   in
As   they   at   the   Parsonage building came   crept   Daumesdick   in
                                                                   (Thumbthick)

die   Kammer,   schrie   aber   gleich   aus   Leibeskräften;   "wollt
the   room   cried   however   directly   out   body forces   want
                                                          (of all might)

ihr   alles   haben,   was   hier   ist?"
you   everything have   what   here   is

Die   Diebe   erschraken   und   sagten;   "so   sprich   doch
The   thieves   frightened   and   said   so   speak   but

leise,   damit   niemand   aufwacht."
quietly   therewith   nobody   wakes up
           (so that)

Aber   Daumesdick   tat,   als   hätte   er   sie   nicht   verstanden,
But   Daumesdick   did   as if   had   he   them   not   understood , heard
         (Thumbthick)

und   schrie   von   neuem: "Was   wollt   ihr?   Wollt   ihr   alles
and   cried   again   What   (do) want you   Want   you   everything

haben,   was   hier   ist?"
have   what   here   is

Das	hörte	die	Köchin,	die	in	der	Stube	daran	schlief,
That	heard	the	cook	that	in	the	little room	next to it	slept

richtete	sich	im	Bett	auf	und	horchte.	Die	Diebe	aber
rose	herself	in the	bed	up	and	listened intently	The	thieves	however

waren	vor	Schrecken	ein	Stück	Wegs	zurückgelaufen,
were (had)	of	fright	a	little	way	run back

endlich	faßten	sie	wieder	Mut	und	dachten	"der	kleine
finally	seized	they	again	courage	and	thought	the	small

Kerl	will	uns	necken."
chap	wants	of us	make a fool

Sie	kamen	zurück	und	flüsterten	ihm	zu"nun	mach
They	came	back	and	whispered	him	to now	do (act)

Ernst	und	reich	uns	etwas	heraus."
serious (seriously)	and	hand	us	something	out

Da	schrie	Daumesdick	noch	einmal,	so	laut	er	konnte;
There	cried	Daumesdick (Thumbthick)	still	once more	so	loud	he	could

"ich	will	euch	ja	alles	geben,	reicht	nur	die	Hände
I	want	you	yes	everything	give	reach	only	the	hands

herein."
in here

63 Daumesdick

Das / hörte / die / horchende / Magd / ganz / deutlich, / sprang
That / heard / the / carefully listening / maid / very / clear / jumped

aus / dem / Bett / und / stolperte / zur / Tür / herein. / Die / Diebe
out of / the / bed / and / stumbled / to the / door / through / The / thieves

liefen / fort / und / rannten, / als / wäre / der / wilde / Jäger
ran / away / and / ran / as if / were / the / wild / hunter

hinter / ihnen; / die / Magd / aber, / als / sie / nichts / bemerken
after / them / the / maid / however / as / she / nothing / notice

konnte, / ging / ein / Licht / anzünden. / Wie / sie / damit
could / went / a / light / to ignite / As / she / with it

herbeikam, / machte / sich / Daumesdick, / ohne / daß / er
came along / made / himself / Daumesdick / without / that / he
(Thumbthick)

gesehen / wurde, / hinaus / in / die / Scheune: / die / Magd / aber,
seen / became / outside / in / the / barn / the / maid / however
(was)

nachdem / sie / alle / Winkel / durchgesucht / und / nichts
after / she / every / corner / searched / and / nothing

gefunden / hatte, / legte / sich / endlich / wieder / zu / Bett / und
found / had / put / herself / finally / again / to / bed / and

glaubte, / sie / hätte / mit / offenen / Augen / und / Ohren / doch
believed / she / had / with / open / eyes / and / ears / just

nur / geträumt.
only / dreamed

Daumesdick war in den Heuhälmchen herumgeklettert und
Daumesdick was in the hay climbed and
(Thumbthick)

hatte einen schönen Platz zum Schlafen gefunden: da
had a beautiful place to sleep found there

wollte er sich ausruhen, bis es Tag wäre, und dann
wanted he himself rest until it day would be and then

zu seinen Eltern wieder heimgehen.
to his parents again go home

Aber er mußte andere Dinge erfahren! ja, es gibt viel
But he had other things to experience yes it gives much

Trübsal und Not auf der Welt! Die Magd stieg, als
affliction and distress on the world The maid rose as

der Tag graute, schon aus dem Bett, um das Vieh
the day became grey already from the bed for the cattle
(dawned)

zu füttern. Ihr erster Gang war in die Scheune, wo
to feed Her first trip was into the barn where

sie einen Arm voll Heu packte, und gerade dasjenige,
she one arm full hay gathered and exactly that

worin der arme Daumesdick lag und schlief.
where the poor Daumesdick lay and slept
(Thumbthick)

65 Daumesdick

Er	schlief	aber	so	fest,	daß	er	nichts	gewahr	ward,
He	slept	however	so	sound	that	he	(of) nothing	aware	became

und	nicht	eher	aufwachte,	als	bis	er	in	dem	Maul
and	not	before	woke up	as	until	he	in	the	muzzle

der	Kuh	war,	die	ihn	mit	dem	Heu	aufgerafft	hatte.
of the	cow	was	that	him	with	the	hay	picked up	had

"Ach	Gott,"	rief	er,	"wie	bin	ich	in	die	Walkmühle
Oh	God	called	he	how	am	I	in	the	press mill

geraten!"	merkte	aber	bald,	wo	er	war.	Da	hieß	es
gotten	noticed	however	soon	where	he	was	There	called	it (meant)

aufpassen,	daß	er	nicht	zwischen	die	Zähne	kam	und
to watch out	that	he	not	between	the	teeth	came	and

zermalmt	ward,	und	hernach	mußte	er	doch	mit	in
crushed	became	and	after that	had to	he	nonetheless	with	in (the hay)

den	Magen	hinabrutschen.	"In	dem	Stübchen	sind	die
the	stomach	slip down	In	the	little room	are	the

Fenster	vergessen,"	sprach	er,	"und	scheint	keine	Sonne
windows	forgotten	spoke	he	and	shines	no	sun

hinein:	ein	Licht	wird	auch	nicht	gebracht."
in	a	light	becomes	also	not	brought
			(is)			

Überhaupt	gefiel	ihm	das	Quartier	schlecht,	und	was
In any way	pleased	him	the	accommodation	badly	and	what

das	Schlimmste	war,	es	kam	immer	mehr	neues	Heu
the	worst	was	it (there)	came	always	more	new	hay

zur Türe	hinein,	und	der	Platz	ward	immer	enger.	Da
through the door	inside	and	the	place	became	always	smaller	Then

rief	er	endlich	in	der	Angst,	so	laut	er	konnte,
called	he	finally	in	(the)	fear	so	loud	he	could

"Bringt	mir	kein	frisch	Futter	mehr,	bringt	mir	kein
Bring	me	no	fresh	fodder	(any) more	bring	me	no

frisch	Futter	mehr."
fresh	fodder	(any) more

Die	Magd	melkte	gerade	die	Kuh,	und	als	sie
The	maid	milked	just	the	cow	and	as	she

sprechen	hörte,	ohne	jemand	zu	sehen,	und	es
speaking	heard	without	someone	to	see	and	it

dieselbe	Stimme	war,	die	sie	auch	in	der	Nacht
the same	voice	was	that	she	also	in	the	night

gehört	hatte,	erschrak	sie	so,	daß	sie	von	ihrem
heard	had	frightened	she	so	that	she	of	her

Stühlchen	herabglitschte	und	die	Milch	verschüttete.
little stool	slipped	and	the	Milk	spilled

Sie	lief	in	der	größten	Hast	zu	ihrem	Herrn	und	rief:
She	ran	in	the	largest	haste	to	her	employer	and	called

"Ach	Gott,	Herr	Pfarrer,	die	Kuh	hat	geredet."
Oh	God	Sir	Minister (religious)	the	cow	has	talked

"Du	bist	verrückt,"	antwortete	der	Pfarrer,	ging	aber
You	are	crazy	answered	the	Minister	went	however

doch	selbst	in	den	Stall	und	wollte	nachsehen,	was
nevertheless	self	in	the	stable	and	wanted	to check	what

es	da	gäbe.	Kaum	aber	hatte	er	den	Fuß
it	there	would give (have)	Hardly	however	had	he	the	foot

hineingesetzt,	so	rief	Daumesdick	aufs	neue:	"Bringt	mir
set in	so	called	Daumesdick (Thumbthick)	again		Bring	me

kein	frisch	Futter	mehr,	bringt	mir	kein	frisch	Futter
no	fresh	fodder	(any) more	bring	me	no	fresh	fodder

mehr."
(any) more

Da	erschrak	der	Pfarrer	selbst,	meinte,	es	wäre	ein
There	frightened	the	Minister	even	meant	it (there)	was	an

böser	Geist	in	die	Kuh	gefahren,	und	hieß	sie	töten.
evil	spirit	in	the	cow	moved	and	had	her	kill (killed)

Sie	ward	geschlachtet,	der	Magen	aber,	worin
She	became	slaughtered	the	stomach	however	where
	(was)					

Daumesdick	steckte,	auf	den	Mist	geworfen.	Daumesdick
Daumesdick	stuck	on	the	dung	thrown	Daumesdick
(Thumbthick)				(heap)		(Thumbthick)

hatte	große	Mühe,	sich	hindurchzuarbeiten,	und	hatte
had	large	trouble	himself	to work through	and	had

große	Mühe	damit,	doch	brachte	er's	so	weit,	daß	er
large	trouble	with it	but	brought	he it	so	far	that	he

Platz	bekam,	aber	als	er	eben	sein	Haupt
room	got	but	as	he	even	his	head

herausstrecken	wollte,	kam	ein	neues	Unglück.	Ein
stick out	wanted	came	a	new	misfortune	A

hungriger	Wolf	lief	heran	und	verschlang	den	ganzen
hungry	wolf	walked	by	and	devoured	the	whole

Magen	mit	einem	Schluck.
stomach	with	one	gulp
	(in)		

Daumesdick	verlor	den	Mut	nicht,	"vielleicht,"	dachte	er,
Daumesdick	lost	(the)	courage	not	perhaps	thought	he
(Thumbthick)							

"läßt	der	Wolf	mit	sich	reden,"	und	rief	ihm	aus	dem
lets	the	wolf	with	itself	talk	and	called	to it	out	the

Wanste	zu;	"lieber	Wolf,	ich	weiß	dir	einen	herrlichen
belly	(to)	dear	wolf	I	know	you	a	wonderful

Fraß."
food

"Wo ist der zu holen?" sprach der Wolf.
Where is that to get said the wolf

"In dem und dem Haus, da mußt du durch die
In this and that house then must you through the

Gosse hineinkriechen, und wirst Kuchen, Speck und
gutter creep in and will cake bacon and

Wurst finden, so viel du essen willst," und beschrieb
sausage find so much you eat want and described

ihm genau seines Vaters Haus.
it exactly his father's house

Der Wolf ließ sich das nicht zweimal sagen, drängte
The wolf let itself that not twice say pushed

sich in der Nacht zur Gosse hinein und fraß in der
itself in the night into the gutter inside and ate in the

Vorratskammer nach Herzenslust. Als er sich gesättigt
store after heart's desire As it itself satisfied

hatte "wollte er wieder fort, aber er war so dick
had wanted it again (to go) away but it was so fat

geworden" daß er denselben Weg nicht wieder hinaus
become that it the same way not again outside

konnte.
could

71 Daumesdick

Darauf hatte Daumesdick gerechnet und fing nun an in
On that had Daumesdick counted and caught now on in
(Thumbthick) [started now]

dem Leib des Wolfes einen gewaltigen Lärmen zu
the body of the wolf an enormous racket to

machen, tobte und schrie, was er konnte.
make raved and cried what he could

"Willst du stille sein," sprach der Wolf, "du weckst die
Want you quiet be spoke the wolf you wake the

Leute auf."
people up

"Ei was," antwortete der Kleine, "du hast dich satt
So what answered the small one you have yourself full

gefressen, ich will mich auch lustig machen," und fing
eaten I want me also fun to make and caught
[started

von neuem an, aus allen Kräften zu schreien. Davon
from new on out of all powers to scream Of that
again] (with)

erwachte endlich sein Vater und seine Mutter, liefen an
woke finally his father and his mother, ran on
(to)

die Kammer und schauten durch die Spalte hinein.
the room and looked through the gap inside

Wie sie sahen, daß ein Wolf darin hauste, liefen sie
As they saw that a wolf therein resided ran they

davon, und der Mann holte eine Axt, und die Frau
(away) from there and the man got an axe and the woman

die Sense.
the scythe

"Bleib dahinten," sprach der Mann, als sie in die
Stay back spoke the man as they in the

Kammer traten, "wenn ich ihm einen Schlag gegeben
room stepped if I it a blow given

habe, und er davon noch nicht tot ist, so mußt du
have and he of it still not dead is so must you

auf ihn einhauen, und ihm den Leib zerschneiden."
on it hack and it the body cut

Da hörte Daumesdick die Stimme seines Vaters und
There heard Daumesdick the voice of his father and
(Thumbthick)

rief "lieber Vater, ich bin hier, ich stecke im Leibe
called dear father I am here I am stuck in the body

des Wolfs."
of the wolf

73 Daumesdick

Sprach der Vater voll Freuden: "Gottlob, unser liebes
Said / the / father / full (of) / joy / praise God / our / dear

Kind hat sich wiedergefunden," und hieß die Frau die
child / has / himself / recovered / and / had / the / wife / the

Sense wegtun, damit Daumesdick nicht beschädigt würde.
scythe / do away / so that / Daumesdick (Thumbthick) / not / hurt / became (would be)

Danach holte er aus, und schlug dem Wolf einen
Afterwards / got (hit) / he / out / and / struck / the / wolf / a

Schlag auf den Kopf, daß er tot niederstürzte, dann
blow / on / the / head / (so) that / it / dead / fell down / then

suchten sie Messer und Schere, schnitten ihm den
searched / they / knives / and / shears / cut / it / the

Leib auf und zogen den Kleinen wieder hervor.
body / up / and / pulled / the / small one / again / out

"Ach," sprach der Vater, "was haben wir für Sorge um
Oh / spoke / the / father / what / have / we / for / worries / over

dich ausgestanden!"
you / stood out (had)

"Ja, Vater, ich bin viel in der Welt herumgekommen;
Yes Father I am much in the world come around
(have)

gottlob, daß ich wieder frische Luft schöpfe!"
praise god that I again fresh Air inhale

"Wo bist du denn all gewesen?"
Where are you then all been
(have) (everywhere)

"Ach, Vater, ich war in einem Mauseloch, in einer Kuh
Oh Father I was in a mouse hole in a cow
('s)

Bauch und in eines Wolfes Wanst: nun bleib ich bei
belly and in a wolf's tummy now stay I with

euch."
you

"Und wir verkaufen dich um alle Reichtümer der Welt
And we sell you for all wealth of the world

nicht wieder," sprachen die Eltern, herzten und küßten
not again said the parents hugged and kissed

ihren lieben Daumesdick.
their dear Daumesdick
(Thumbthick)

Sie   gaben   ihm   zu   essen   und   trinken,   und   ließen   ihm
They   gave   him   to   eat   and   drink   and   let   for him

neue   Kleider   machen,   denn   die   seinigen   waren   ihm   auf
new   clothing   make   because   those   of his   were   him   on

der   Reise   verdorben.
the   journey   spoiled

77   Daumesdick

DIE   GÄNSEMAGD
THE   GOOSE MAID

Es lebte einmal eine alte Königin, der war ihr Gemahl
It lived once an old queen of who was her husband
(There)

schon lange Jahre gestorben, und sie hatte eine
already long years dead and she had a

schöne Tochter. Wie die erwuchs, wurde sie weit über
beautiful daughter As she grew up became she far over
[far away

Feld an einen Königssohn versprochen. Als nun die
field to a king's son promised As now the
]

Zeit kam, wo sie vermählt werden sollten und das
time came where she in wedlock become should and the
(go)

Kind in das fremde Reich abreisen mußte, packte ihr
child into the strange land leave had packed her

die Alte gar viel köstliches Gerät und Geschmeide ein,
the old one well much expensive materials and jewelry a

Gold und Silber, Becher und Kleinode, kurz alles, was
gold and silver cup and jewels briefly everything what

nur zu einem königlichen Brautschatz gehörte, denn sie
only to a royal dowry belonged because she

hatte ihr Kind von Herzen lieb.
had her child of heart dear
(heartily)

Auch	gab	sie	ihr	eine	Kammerjungfer	bei,	welche
Also	gave	she	her	a	chambermaid	(by)	who

mitreiten	und	die	Braut	in	die	Hände	des	Bräutigams
ride along	and	the	bride	in	the	hands	of the	bridegroom

überliefern	sollte,	und	jede	bekam	ein	Pferd	zur	Reise,
deliver	should	and	everyone	got	on	horse	for the	journey

aber	das	Pferd	der	Königstochter	hieß	Falada	und
but	the	horse	of the	king's daughter	was called	Falada	and

konnte	sprechen.	Wie	nun	die	Abschiedsstunde	da	war,
could	speak	As	now	the	parting hour	there	was

begab	sich	die	alte	Mutter	in	ihre	Schlafkammer,	nahm
went	herself	the	old	mother	into	their	sleeping chamber	took

ein	Messerlein	und	schnitt	damit	in	ihre	Finger,	daß
a	little knife	and	cut	with it	in	her	fingers	that

sie	bluteten:
they	bled

Darauf	hielt	sie	ein	weißes	Läppchen	unter	und	ließ
whereupon	held	she	a	white	small cloth	under (them)	and	let

drei	Tropfen	Blut	hineinfallen,	gab	sie	der	Tochter	und
three	drops	(of) blood	fall	gave	it	the	daughter	and

sprach:
spoke

81 Die Gänsemagd

"Liebes Kind, verwahre sie wohl, sie werden dir
Dear child keep it well they will you

unterwegs nicht tun."
on the way harm do

Also nahmen beide voneinander betrübten Abschied: das
Thus took both from each other sad leave the

Läppchen steckte die Königstochter in ihren Busen vor
small cloth put the king's daughter in her bosom for

sich, setzte sich aufs Pferd und zog nun fort zu
herself set herself on the horse and pulled now away to
(set) (off)

ihrem Bräutigam. Da sie eine Stunde geritten waren,
her bridegroom Then they one hour ridden were
(When) (had)

empfand sie heißen Durst und sprach zu ihrer
felt she hot thirst and said to her
(extreme)

Kammerjungfer:
chamber maid

"Steig ab, und schöpfe mir mit meinem Becher, den
Mount off and scoop me with my cup that
(Dismount)

du für mich mitgenommen hast, Wasser aus dem
you for me taken along have water out of the

Bache, ich möchte gern einmal trinken."
brook I would like gladly one time drink
(stream)

83 Die Gänsemagd

"Wenn Ihr Durst habt," sprach die Kammerjungfer, "so
If you thirst have said the chamber maid so
(thirsty are)

steigt selber ab, legt Euch ans Wasser und trinkt, ich
mount yourself (off) lay yourself to the water and drink I
(absteigen; dismount)

mag Eure Magd nicht sein."
like your maid not be

Da stieg die Königstochter vor großem Durst herunter,
There rose the king's daughter of great thirst down
(stieg herunter; came down)

neigte sich über das Wasser im Bach und trank, und
lied herself over the water in the brook and drank and
(to)

durfte nicht aus dem goldenen Becher trinken.
was allowed not out of the golden cup to drink

Da sprach sie, "Ach Gott!" und da antworteten die
There spoke she Oh God and there answered the

drei Blutstropfen:
three blood drops

"Wenn das deine Mutter wüßte,
If that your mother would know

Das Herz im Leibe tät ihr zerspringen."
The heart in the body did of her shatter
(would)

Aber die Königsbraut war demütig, sagte nichts und
But the king's bride was humble said nothing and

stieg wieder zu Pferde.
mounted again onto horse

So ritten sie etliche Meilen weiter fort, aber der Tag
So rode they some miles further forth but the day

war warm, die Sonne stach, und sie durstete bald
was warm the sun stung and she thirsted soon

von neuem.
of new
(again)

Da sie nun an einen Wasserfluß kamen, rief sie noch
There they now by a river came called she still

einmal ihrer Kammerjungfer:
once more her chamber maid

"Steig ab und gib mir aus meinem Goldbecher zu
Rise off and give me out of my gold cup to
(Dismount)

trinken," denn sie hatte aller bösen Worte längst
drink because she had all bad words already long

vergessen.
forgotten

85 Die Gänsemagd

Die Kammerjungfer sprach aber noch hochmütiger:
The chamber maid spoke however even more arrogantly

"Wollt Ihr trinken, so trinkt allein, ich mag nicht Eure
Want you drink so drink however I like not your

Magd sein."
maid be

Da stieg die Königstochter hernieder vor großem Durst,
Then rose the king's daughter down in great thirst
(climbed)

legte sich über das fließende Wasser, weinte und
bent herself over the flowing water cried and

sprach, "Ach Gott!" und die Blutstropfen antworteten
spoke Oh God and the blood drops answered

wiederum:
again

"Wenn das deine Mutter wüßte,
If that your mother would know

Das Herz im Leibe tät ihr zerspringen."
The heart in the body did it shatter
(would)

Und wie sie so trank und sich recht überlehnte, fiel
And as she thus drank and herself completely leaned over fell

ihr das Läppchen, worin die drei Tropfen waren, aus
of her the small cloth in which the three drops were out of

dem Busen und floß mit dem Wasser fort, ohne daß
the bosom and flowed with the water away without that

sie es in ihrer großen Angst merkte.
she it in her large fear noticed

Die Kammerjungfer hatte aber zugesehen und freute
The chamber maid had however watched and was pleased

sich, daß sie Gewalt über die Braut bekäme: denn
herself that she power over the bride would get because

damit, daß diese die Blutstropfen verloren hatte, war
thus that this one the blood drops lost had was

sie schwach und machtlos geworden.
she weak and powerless become

Als sie nun wieder auf ihr Pferd steigen wollte, das
As she now again up on her horse rise wanted that
(mount)

da hieß Falada, sagte die Kammerfrau:
there was called Falada said the chamber maid

"Auf   Falada   gehör   ich,   und   auf   meinen   Gaul   gehörst
On   Falada   belong I   and   on   my   nag   belong

du ; "   und   das   mußte   sie   sich   gefallen   lassen.
you   and   that had to she   herself befall   let
                                          (happen)

Dann   befahl   ihr   die   Kammerfrau   mit   harten   Worten,   die
Then   ordered her   the   chamber maid with severe   words   the

königlichen   Kleider   auszuziehen   und   ihre   schlechten
royal   dresses   to take off   and   her   bad ones
                                            (own)

anzulegen,   und   endlich   mußte   sie   sich   unter   freiem
to put on   and   in the end had   she   herself under   open

Himmel   verschwören,   daß   sie   am   königlichen   Hof
sky   to swear   that she   at the royal   court

keinem   Menschen   etwas   davon   sprechen   wollte;   und
no   man   anything of it   tell   would   and

wenn   sie   diesen   Eid   nicht   abgelegt   hätte,   wäre   sie
if   she   this   oath   not   laid off   would have would be   she
                                     (taken)

auf   der   Stelle   umgebracht   worden.   Aber   Falada   sah
on   the   spot   killed   be   But   Falada   looked

das   alles   an   und   nahm's   wohl   in   acht.
it   all   at   and   took it   well   in   consideration

Die   Kammerfrau   stieg   nun   auf   Falada   und   die   wahre
The   chamber maid   climbed   now   on   Falada   and   the   true

Braut   auf   das   schlechte   Roß,   und   so   zogen   sie
bride   on   the   bad   horse   and   so   drew   they
                                                                    (travelled)

weiter,   bis   sie   endlich   in   dem   königlichen   Schloß
further   until   they   finally   in   the   royal   castle

eintrafen.
arrived

Da   war   große   Freude   über   ihre   Ankunft,   und   der
There   was   large   joy   over   their   arrival   and   the

Königssohn   sprang   ihnen   entgegen,   hob   die   Kammerfrau
king's son   leaped   them   before   lifted   the   chamber maid

vom   Pferde   und   meinte,   sie   wäre   seine   Gemahlin: sie
of the   horse   and   thought   she   were   his   wife   she

ward   die   Treppe   hinaufgeführt,   die   wahre   Königstochter
became   the   stairs   led up   the   true   king's daughter

aber   mußte   unten   stehen   bleiben.
however   had to   down   stand   remain
                      (stairs)

89 Die Gänsemagd

Da schaute der alte König am Fenster und sah sie
Then looked the old king by the window and saw her

im Hof halten und sah, wie sie fein war, zart und
in the yard wait and saw how she fine was tender and

gar schön: ging alsbald hin ins königliche Gemach und
quite beautiful went immediately into in the royal chamber and

fragte die Braut nach der, die sie bei sich hätte und
asked the bride after her that she with herself had and

da unten im Hofe stände, und wer sie wäre.
there down in the courtyard stood and who she were

"Die hab ich mir unterwegs mitgenommen zur
That one have I for me on the way taken along as

Gesellschafe; gebe der Magd was zu arbeiten, daß sie
company give the maid something to work that she

nicht müßig stehe."
not idle stands

Aber der alte König hatte keine Arbeit für sie und
But the old king had no work for her and

wußte nichts, als daß er sagte:
knew nothing as that he said

"Da hab ich so einen kleinen Jungen, der hütet die
There have I so a small boy who looks after the

Gänse, dem mag sie helfen." Der Junge hieß Kürdchen
geese that one may she help The boy was called

(Konrädchen), dem mußte die wahre Braut helfen Gänse
that one had the true bride to help geese

hüten.
look after

Bald aber sprach die falsche Braut zu dem jungen
Soon however spoke the false bride to the young

König "liebster Gemahl, ich bitte Euch, tut mir einen
king dearest husband I ask you do me one

Gefallen."
Favour

Er antwortete"das will ich gerne tun."
He answered that shall I gladly do

"Nun so laßt den Schinder rufen und da dem Pferde,
Now so let the skinner call and there that horse
(butcher)

worauf ich hergeritten bin, den Hals abhauen, weil es
on which I here ridden are the neck chop off because it
(was)

mich unterwegs geärgert hat."
me on the way annoyed has

Eigentlich aber fürchtete sie, daß das Pferd sprechen
In reality however was afraid she that the horse speak

möchte, wie sie mit der Königstochter umgegangen war.
might how she with the king's daughter gone around was (had)

Nun war das so weit geraten, daß es geschehen und
Now was it so far gotten that it happen and

der treue Falada sterben sollte, da kam es auch der
the faithful Falada die should there came it also the

rechten Königstochter zu Ohr, und sie versprach dem
true king's daughter to (her) ear (attention) and she promised the

Schinder heimlich ein Stück Geld, das sie ihm
flayer (butcher) secretly a part (heap of) money that she him

bezahlen wollte, wenn er ihr einen kleinen Dienst
pay would if he her a small service

erwiese. In der Stadt war ein großes finsteres Tor, wo
would provide In the city was a large dark gate where

sie abends und morgens mit den Gänsen durch mußte,
she in the evening and in the morning with the geese through had to

unter das finstere Tor möchte er dem Falada seinen
under the dark gate could he (the) Falada his

Kopf hinnageln, daß sie ihn doch noch mehr als
head nail that she it but still more as

einmal sehen könnte.
once see could

93 Die Gänsemagd

Also	versprach	das	der	Schindersknecht		zu	tun,	hieb
Thus	promised	it	the	butcher servant		to	do	chopped

den	Kopf	ab	und	nagelte	ihn	unter	das	finstere	Tor
the	head	off	and	nailed	it	under	the	dark	gate

fest.
down

Des	Morgens	früh,	da	sie	und	Kürdchen	unterm	Tor
In the	morning	early	then (when)	she	and	little Kurd	under the	gate

hinaustrieben,	sprach	sie	im	Vorbeigehen:
drove out	spoke	she	in the	passing

"O	du	Falada,	da	du	hangest!"
O	you	Falada	there	you	hang

Da	antwortete	der	Kopf:
There	answered	the	head

"O	du	Jungfer	Königin,	da	du	gangest,
O	you	maiden	queen	there	you	go

Wenn	das	deine	Mutter	wüßte
If	that	your	mother	would know

ihr	Herz	tät	ihr	zerspringen."
her	heart	would do it		shatter (break)

Da zog sie still weiter zur Stadt hinaus, und sie
There drew she even further on the city outside and they

trieben die Gänse aufs Feld. Und wenn sie auf der
drove the geese on the field And when they on the
(into the) (countryside)

Wiese angekommen war, saß sie nieder und machte
meadow arrived were sat she down and made
(had)

ihre Haare auf, die waren eitel Gold, und Kürdchen
her hair up they were pure gold and little Kurd

sah sie und freute sich, wie sie und wollte ihr ein
saw them and was pleased himself as her and wanted of her a

paar ausraufen. Da sprach sie:
few to rob There spoke she
(pull out)

"Weh, weh, Windchen,
Blow blow little wind

Nimm Kürdchen sein Hütchen,
Take little Kurd his little hat

Und laß'n sich mit jagen,
And let it himself to chase after

Bis ich mich geflochten und geschnatzt,
Until I myself braided and arranged

Und wieder aufgesatzt."
And again touched up
(made up)

95 Die Gänsemagd

Und	da	kam	ein	so	starker	Wind,	daß	er	dem
And	there	came	a	so	strong	wind	that	it	(the)

Kürdchen	sein	Hütchen	wegwehte	über	alle	Land,	und
little Kurd	his	little hat	blew away	over	the whole	countryside	and

es	mußte	ihm	nachlaufen.
it	had	it	to run after
(he)			

Bis	es	wiederkam,	war	sie	mit	dem	Kämmen	und
Until	it	came back	was	she	with	the	combing	and
(When)	(he)							

Aufsetzen	fertig,	und	er	konnte	keine	Haare	kriegen.
touching up	finished	and	he	could	no	hair	get
(making up)							

Da	war	Kürdchen	bös	und	sprach	nicht	mit	ihr;	und
Then	was	little Kurd	angry	and	spoke	not	with	her	and

so	hüteten	sie	die	Gänse,	bis	daß	es	Abend	ward,
so	tended	they	the	geese	until	that	it	evening	became

dann	gingen	sie	nach	Haus.
then	went	they	home	

Den	andern	Morgen,	wie	sie	unter	dem	finstern	Tor
The	other	morning,	as	they	under	the	dark	gate
	(next)							

hinaustrieben,	sprach	die	Jungfrau:
drove out	spoke	the	maiden

97 Die Gänsemagd

"O du Falada, da du hangest!"
O you Falada, there you hang

Falada antwortete:
Falada answered

"O du Jungfer Königin, da du gangest,
O you maiden queen, there you go

Wenn das deine Mutter wüßte
If that your mother would know

ihr Herz tät ihr zerspringen."
her heart would it shatter
(break)

Und in dem Feld setzte sie sich wieder auf die
And in the field set she herself again up on the
(countryside)

Wiese und fing an ihr Haar auszukämmen, und
meadow and started her hair to comb out and

Kürdchen lief und wollte danach greifen, da sprach sie
Kurd ran up and wanted to it grasp then spoke she

schnell:
quickly

"Weh,   weh,   Windchen,
Blow   blow   little wind

Nimm   Kürdchen   sein   Hütchen,
Take   little Kurd   his   Hat

Und   laß'n   sich   mit   jagen,
And   let him   itself   chase off

Bis   ich   mich   geflochten   und   geschnatzt,
Until   I   myself   braided   and   arranged

Und   wieder   aufgesatzt."
And   again   touched up
(made up)

Da   wehte   der   Wind   und   wehte   ihm   das   Hütchen   vom
Then   blew   the   wind   and   blew   him   the   little hat   from the

Kopf   weit   weg,   daß   Kürdchen   nachlaufen   mußte;   und
head   far   away   (so) that   little Kurd   to run after   had   and

als   es   wiederkam,   hatte   sie   längst   ihr   Haar   zurecht,
as   he   came back   had   she   already long   her   hair   straightened out

und   es   konnte   keins   davon   erwischen;   und   so   hüteten
and   it   could   none   of it   get   and   so   tended
(he)   (steal)

sie   die   Gänse,   bis   es   Abend   ward.   Abends   aber,
they   the   geese   until   it   evening   became   In the evening   however

nachdem   sie   heim   gekommen   waren,   ging   Kürdchen   vor
after   they   home   come   were   went   little Kurd   before

den   alten   König   und   sagte:
the   old   king   and   said

99 Die Gänsemagd

"Mit dem Mädchen will ich nicht länger Gänse hüten."
With that girl want I not (any) longer geese look after

"Warum denn?" fragte der alte König.
Why then asked the old king

"Ei, das ärgert mich den ganzen Tag."
Well that annoys me the whole day
(she) (it)

Da befahl ihm der alte König zu erzählen, wie's ihm
Then ordered him the old king to tell how it him

denn mit ihr ginge.
then with her went

Da sagte Kürdchen, "Morgens, wenn wir unter dem
Then said little Kurd In the morning when we under the

finsteren Tor mit der Herde durchkommen, so ist da
dark gate with the flock come through so is there

ein Gaulskopf an der Wand, zu dem redet sie:"
a horses head on the wall to it talks she

101 Die Gänsemagd

'"O du Falada, da du hangest,' und da antwortet der
O you Falada there you hang and then answers the

Kopf, 'O du Jungfer Königin, da du gangest,
head O you maiden queen there you go

Wenn das deine Mutter wüßte
If that your mother would know

ihr Herz tät ihr zerspringen.'"
her heart would her shatter
              (break)

Und so erzählte Kürdchen weiter, was auf der
And so told little Kurd on what on the

Gänsewiese geschähe, und wie es da dem Hut im
goose meadow would happen and how it there the hat in the
                                    (he)

Winde nachlaufen müßte.
wind run after would have to

Der alte König befahl ihm, den nächsten Tag wieder
The old king instructed him the next day again

hinauszutreiben, und er selbst, wie es Morgen war,
to drive out and he himself as it morning was

setzte sich hinter das finstere Tor und hörte da, wie
set himself behind the dark gate and heard there how

sie mit dem Haupt des Falada sprach:
she with the head of the Falada spoke

102　Die Gänsemagd

und	dann	ging	er	ihr	auch	nach	in	das	Feld	und
and	then	went	he	her	also	after	in	the	field	and

barg	sich	in	einem	Busch	auf	der	Wiese.
hid	himself	in	a	bush	on	the	meadow

Da	sah	er	nun	bald	mit	seinen	eigenen	Augen,	wie
There	saw	he	now	soon	with	his	own	eyes	how

die	Gänsemagd	und	der	Gänsejunge	die	Herde
the	goose maid	and	the	goose boy	the	flock

getrieben	brachte,	und	wie	nach	einer	Weile	sie	sich
driving	brought	and	how	after	a	while	she	herself

setzte	und	ihre	Haare	losflocht,	die	strahlten	von	Glanz.
sat down	and	her	hair	twisted loose	which	radiated	of	gloss (shine)

Gleich	sprach	sie	wieder:
Directly	spoke	she	again

103 Die Gänsemagd

"Weh, weh, Windchen,
Blow blow little wind

Nimm Kürdchen sein Hütchen,
Take little Kurd his little hat

Und laß'n sich mit jagen,
And let him itself chase off

Bis ich mich geflochten und geschnatzt,
Until I myself braided and arranged

Und wieder aufgesatzt."
And again touched up
(made up)

Da kam ein Windstoß und fuhr mit Kürdchens Hut
There came a gust of wind and blew with little Kurd's hat

weg, daß es weit zu laufen hatte, und die Magd
away that it far to run had and the maid
(he)

kämmte und flocht ihre Locken still fort, welches der
combed and braided her curls quietly on of which the

alte König alles beobachtete. Darauf ging er unbemerkt
old king all observed Whereupon went he unnoticed

zurück, und als abends die Gänsemagd heim kam, rief
back and as in the evening the goose maid home came called

er sie beiseite und fragte, warum sie dem allem so
he her aside and asked why she that all so

täte.
would do

"Das darf ich Euch nicht sagen, und darf auch
That may I you not tell and may also

keinem Menschen mein Leid klagen, denn so hab ich
no human my suffering complain because so have I
(one)

mich unter freiem Himmel verschworen, weil ich sonst
myself under open sky sworn because I otherwise

um mein Leben gekommen wäre."
for my Life come were
(um das Leben kommen: to lose one's life)

Er drang in sie und ließ ihr keinen Frieden, aber er
He pushed on her and left her no peace but he

konnte nichts aus ihr herausbringen.
could nothing out of her get out

Da sprach er:
Then spoke he

"Wenn du mir's nicht sagen willst, so klag dem
If you me it not say will so complain to the

Eisenofen da dein Leid," und ging fort.
iron furnace then your suffering and went away

105 Die Gänsemagd

Da kroch sie in den Eisenofen, fing an zu jammern
There crept she in the iron furnace started to lament

und zu weinen, schüttete ihr Herz aus und sprach:
and to cry poured her heart out and spoke

"Da sitze ich nun von aller Welt verlassen, und bin
There sit I now of all world left and am
(by)

doch eine Königstochter, und eine falsche Kammerjungfer
nevertheless a king's daughter and a false chamber maid

hat mich mit Gewalt dahingebracht, daß ich meine
has me with force brought there that I my
(gotten to)

königlichen Kleider habe ablegen müssen, und hat
royal dresses have taken off had to and has

meinen Platz bei meinem Bräutigam eingenommen, und
my place by my bridegroom taken and

ich muß als Gänsemagd gemeine Dienste tun. Wenn
I must as goose maid common services do If

das meine Mutter wüßte, das Herz im Leib tät ihr
that my mother would know the heart in the body would it

zerspringen."
shatter

Der alte König stand aber außen an der Ofenröhre,
The old king stood however outside by the stove pipe

lauerte ihr zu und hörte, was sie sprach. Da kam er
lurked it next to and heard which she said There came he

wieder herein und hieß sie aus dem Ofen gehen.
again in and had her out of the furnace go

Da wurden ihr königliche Kleider angetan, und es
Then were her royal dresses dressed and it

schien ein Wunder, wie sie so schön war.
seemed a miracle how she so beautiful was

Der alte König rief seinen Sohn und offenbarte ihm,
The old king called his son and revealed him

daß er die falsche Braut hätte: die wäre bloß ein
that he the wrong bride had who was only a

Kammermädchen, die wahre aber stände hier, als die
chamber maid the true however stood here as the

gewesene Gänsemagd.
former goose maid

107 Die Gänsemagd

Der	junge	König	war	herzensfroh,	als	er	ihre	Schönheit
The	young	king	was	glad of heart	as	he	her	beauty

und	Tugend	erblickte,	und	ein	großes	Mahl	wurde
and	virtue	saw	and	a	large	meal	became

angestellt,	zu	dem	alle	Leute	und	guten	Freunde
arranged	to	which	all	people	and	good	friends

gebeten	wurden.	Obenan	saß	der	Bräutigam,	die
asked	became	Above	sat	the	bridegroom	the
[were invited	]					

Königstochter	zur	einen	Seite	und	die	Kammerjungfer
king's daughter	to	one	side	and	the	chamber maid

zur	andern,	aber	die	Kammerjungfer	war	verblendet	und
to the	other one	but	the	chamber maid	was	blinded	and

erkannte	jene	nicht	mehr	in	dem	glänzenden	Schmuck.
recognized	that one	not	(any)more	in	the	shining	adorment

Als	sie	nun	gegessen	und	getrunken	hatten	und	gutes
As	they	now	eaten	and	drunk	had	and	good

Muts	waren,	gab	der	alte	König	der	Kammerfrau	ein
courage	were	gave	the	old	king	the	chamber maid	a

Rätsel	auf,	was	eine	solche	wert	wäre,	die	den	Herrn
riddle	(up)	what	one	such	worth	would be	who	the	lord

so	und	so	betrogen	hätte,	erzählte	damit	den	ganzen
so	and	so	betrayed	would have	told	thus	the	whole

Verlauf	und	fragte:
process	and	asked

"Welches   Urteils   ist   diese   würdig?"
Which   judgement is   this one worthy
                                        (worthy of)

Da   sprach   die   falsche   Braut:
There spoke   the   false   bride

"Die   ist   nichts   Besseres   wert,   als   daß   sie   splitternackt
That one is   no   better   worth   as   that   she   naked

ausgezogen   und   in   ein   Faß   gesteckt   wird,   das
undressed   and   in   a   barrel put   becomes that

inwendig   mit   spitzen   Nägeln   beschlagen   ist: und   zwei
from the inside with sharp   nails   fitted   is   and   two

weiße   Pferde   müssen   vorgespannt   werden,   die   sie
white   horses   must   harnessed   become   which her

Gasse   auf,   Gasse   ab   zu   Tode   schleifen."
lane   up   lane   down to   death   pull

"Das   bist   du,"   sprach   der   alte   König,   "und   hast   dein
That   are   you   spoke   the   old   king   and   have   your

eigen   Urteil   gefunden,   und   danach   soll   dir   widerfahren."
own   judgement found   and   like that will   you   happen

Und als das Urteil vollzogen war, vermählte sich der
And as the judgement carried out was married himself the

junge König mit seiner rechten Gemahlin, und beide
young king with his true wife and both

beherrschten ihr Reich in Frieden und Seligkeit.
ruled their country in peace and bliss

ASCHENPUTTEL
ASCHENPUTTEL

Einem	reichen	Manne,	dem	wurde	seine	Frau	krank,
A	rich	man	of him	became	his	wife	ill

und	als	sie	fühlte,	daß	ihr	Ende	herankam,	rief	sie
and	as	she	felt	that	her	end	approached	called	she

ihr	einziges	Töchterlein	zu	sich	ans	Bett	und	sprach
her	only	little daughter	to	herself	to the	bed	and	spoke

"liebes	Kind,	bleibe	fromm	und	gut,	so	wird	dir	der
dear	child	remain	pious	and	good	so	will	you	the

liebe	Gott	immer	beistehen,	und	ich	will	vom	Himmel
dear	God	always	stand by	and	I	shall	from the	sky

auf	dich	herabblicken,	und	will	um	dich	sein."
on	you	look down	and	shall	over	you	be
(to)					(with)		

Darauf	tat	sie	die	Augen	zu	und	verschied.	Das
Thereupon	did	she	the	eyes	closed	and	passed away	The

Mädchen	ging	jeden	Tag	hinaus	zu	dem	Grabe	der
girl	went	every	day	outside	to	the	grave	of the

Mutter	und	weinte,	und	blieb	fromm	und	gut.
mother	and	cried	and	remained	pious	and	good

Als   der   Winter   kam,   deckte   der   Schnee   ein   weißes
As   the   winter   came   covered   the   snow   a   white

Tüchlein   auf   das   Grab,   und   als   die   Sonne   im
little sheet   over   the   grave   and   as   the   sun   in the

Frühjahr   es   wieder   herabgezogen   hatte,   nahm   sich   der
spring   it   again   pulled away   had   took   himself   the

Mann   eine   andere   Frau.
man   an   other   woman

Die   Frau   hatte   zwei   Töchter   mit   ins   Haus   gebracht,
The   woman   had   two   daughters   along   in the   house   brought

die   schön   und   weiß   von   Angesicht   waren,   aber   garstig
who   beautiful   and   white   of   face   were   but   mean

und   schwarz   von   Herzen.   Da   ging   eine   schlimme   Zeit
and   black   of   heart   There   went   a   bad   time

für   das   arme   Stiefkind   an.   "Soll   die   dumme   Gans   bei
for   the   poor   stepchild   on   Should   that   stupid   goose   with

uns   in   der   Stube   sitzen",   sprachen   sie,   "wer   Brot
us   in   the   room   sit   spoke   they   who   bread

essen   will,   muß   es   verdienen: hinaus   mit   der
eat   wants   must   it   earn   outside   with   the

Küchenmagd."
kitchenmaid

Sie — They
nahmen — took
ihm — her
seine — her
schönen — beautiful
Kleider — dresses
weg, — away
zogen — put

ihm — her
einen — one
grauen — grey
alten — old
Kittel — smock
an, — on
und — and
gaben — gave
ihm — it (her)

hölzerne — wooden
Schuhe. — shoes
"Seht — See
einmal — a time
die — the
stolze — proud
Prinzessin, — princess
wie — how

sie — she
geputzt — polished (dressed up)
ist", — is
riefen — called
sie, — they
lachten — laughed
und — and
führten — led
es — it (her)
in — in

die — the
Küche. — kitchen
Da — There
mußte — had
es — it
von — from
Morgen — morning
bis — to
Abend — evening

schwere — heavy
Arbeit — work
tun, — do
früh — early
vor — before
Tag — day (-break)
aufstehen, — to get up
Wasser — water

tragen, — carry
Feuer — fire
anmachen, — make
kochen — cook
und — and
waschen. — wash
Obendrein — In addition

taten — did
ihm — it (her)
die — the
Schwestern — sisters
alles — all
ersinnliche — thinkable (possible)
Herzeleid — heartache
an, — to

verspotteten — scoffed
es — it (her)
und — and
schütteten — poured
ihm — it (her)
die — the
Erbsen — peas
und — and

Linsen — lentils
in — in
die — the
Asche, — ash (ashes)
so — so
daß — that
es — it (she)
sitzen — sit
und — and
sie — them

wieder — again
auslesen — to select
mußte. — had to

115 Aschenputtel

Abends,	wenn	es	sich	müde	gearbeitet	hatte,	kam	es
In the evening	if	it (she)	itself (herself)	tired	worked	had	came	it (she)

in	kein	Bett,	sondern	mußte	sich	neben	den	Herd	in
in	no	bed	but	had	itself (herself)	beside	the	stove	in

die	Asche	legen.	Und	weil	es	darum	immer	staubig
the	ash (ashes)	to lay	And	because	it (she)	therefore	always	dusty

und	schmutzig	aussah,	nannten	sie	es	Aschenputtel.
and	dirty	looked	called	they	it (her)	Aschenputtel (Cinderella)

Es	trug	sich	zu,	daß	der	Vater	einmal	in	die	Messe
It	happened			that	the	father	once	to	the	market

ziehen	wollte,	da	fragte	er	die	beiden	Stieftöchter,	was
to move	wanted	there	asked	he	the	both	stepdaughters	what

er	ihnen	mitbringen	sollte.
he	for them	bring along	should

"Schöne	Kleider"	sagte	die	eine,	"Perlen	und	Edelsteine"
Beautiful	dresses	said	the	one	Pearls	and	gemstones

die	zweite.
the	second

"Aber du, Aschenputtel" sprach er, "was willst du
But you Aschenputtel spoke he what want you
(Cinderella)

haben?"
to have

"Vater, das erste Reis, das Euch auf Eurem Heimweg
Father the first twig that you on your way home

an den Hut stößt, das brecht für mich ab."
on the hat bumps that break for me off

Er kaufte nun für die beiden Stiefschwestern schöne
He bought now for the both stepsisters beautiful

Kleider, Perlen und Edelsteine, und auf dem Rückweg,
dresses perls and gemstones and on the way back

als er durch einen grünen Busch ritt, streifte ihn ein
as he through some green shrubs rode touched him a

Haselreis und stieß ihm den Hut ab.
twig of hazel and pushed of him the hat off

Da brach er das Reis ab und nahm es mit.
There broke he the twig off and took it with
(him)

Als	er	nach	Haus	kam,	gab	er	den	Stieftöchtern,	was
As	he	to house (home)		came	gave	he	the	stepdaughters	what

sie	sich	gewünscht	hatten,	und	dem	Aschenputtel	gab
they	themselves	wished	had	and	(the)	Aschenputtel (Cinderella)	gave

er	das	Reis	von	dem	Haselbusch.	Aschenputtel	dankte
he	the	twig	of	the	hazelbush	Aschenputtel	thanked

ihm,	ging	zu	seiner	Mutter	Grab	und	pflanzte	das
him	went	to	her	mother's	grave	and	planted	the

Reis	darauf,	und	weinte	so	sehr,	daß	die	Tränen
twig	thereupon	and	cried	so	very much	that	the	tears

darauf	niederfielen	und	es	begossen.	Es	wuchs	aber,
thereupon	fell down	and	it	sprinkled	It	grew	however

und	würde	ein	schöner	Baum.	Aschenputtel	ging	alle
and	became	a	beautiful	tree	Aschenputtel (Cinderella)	went	all

Tage	dreimal	darunter,	weinte	und	betete,	und	allemal
days	three times	under it	cried	and	prayed	and	always

kam	ein	weißes	Vöglein	auf	den	Baum,	und	wenn	es
came	a	white	small bird	up (in)	the	tree	and	if	it (she)

einen	Wunsch	aussprach,	so	warf	ihm	das	Vöglein
a	wish	expressed	so	threw	it (her)	the	small bird

herab,	was	es	sich	gewünscht	hatte.
down	whichever	it (she)	itself (herself)	wished	had

Es	begab	sich	aber,	daß	der	König	ein	Fest	anstellte,
It went	itself		however	that	the	king	a	feast	planned
(It happened)									

das	drei	Tage	dauern	sollte,	und	wozu	alle	schönen
that	three	days	last	should	and	to which	every	beautiful

Jungfrauen	im	Lande	eingeladen	wurden,	damit	sich	sein
maiden	in the	country	invited	became	therewith	himself	his
					(so that)		

Sohn	eine	Braut	aussuchen	möchte.
son	a	bride	select	could

Die	zwei	Stiefschwestern,	als	sie	hörten,	daß	sie	auch
The	two	stepsisters	as	they	heard	that	they	also

dabei	erscheinen	sollten,	waren	guter	Laune,	riefen
there	appear	should	were	in a good	mood	called

Aschenputtel	und	sprachen	"Kämm	uns	die	Haare,
Aschenputtel	and	spoke	Comb	us	the	hairs
(Cinderella)						

bürste	uns	die	Schuhe	und	mache	uns	die	Schnallen
brush	us	the	shoes	and	make	us	the	clasps

fest,	wir	gehen	zur	Hochzeit	auf	des	Königs	Schloß."
fastened	we	go	to	wedding	at	the	king's	castle

Aschenputtel	gehorchte,	weinte	aber,	weil	es	auch	gern
Aschenputtel (Cinderella)	obeyed	cried	however	because	it (she)	also	gladly

zum	Tanz	mitgegangen	wäre,	und	bat	die	Stiefmutter,
to the	dance	gone along	would be (have)	and	asked	the	stepmother

sie	möchte	es	ihm	erlauben.
she	would	it	it (her)	permit

"Du	Aschenputtel"	sprach	sie,	"bist	voll	Staub	und
You	Aschenputtel (Cinderella)	spoke	she	are	full (of)	dust	and

Schmutz,	und	willst	zur	Hochzeit?	du	hast	keine
dirt	and	want	to the	wedding	you	have	no

Kleider	und	Schuhe,	und	willst	tanzen."	Als	es	aber
dresses	and	shoes	and	want	to dance	As	it (she)	however

mit	Bitten	anhielt,	sprach	sie	endlich	"da	habe	ich	dir
with	requests	continued	spoke	she	finally	there	have	I	for you

eine	Schüssel	Linsen	in	die	Asche	geschüttet,	wenn	du
a	dish	lentils	in	the	ashes	poured	if	you

die	Linsen	in	zwei	Stunden	wieder	ausgelesen	hast,	so
the	lentils	in	two	hours	again	sorted out	have	so

sollst	du	mitgehen."
will	you	go along

Das	Mädchen	ging	durch	die	Hintertür	nach	dem
The	girl	went	through	the	back door	to	the

Garten	und	rief,	"ihr	zahmen	Täubchen,	ihr
garden	and	called	you	tame	little doves	you

Turteltäubchen,	all	ihr	Vöglein	unter	dem	Himmel,	kommt
turtledoves	all	you	small birds	under	the	sky	come

und	helft	mir	lesen,
and	help	me	sort

die	guten	ins	Töpfchen,
the	good	in the	little pot

die	schlechten	ins	Kröpfchen."
the	bad	in the	little pouch (crop)

Da	kamen	zum	Küchenfenster	zwei	weiße	Täubchen
There	came	to the	kitchen window	two	white	doves

herein,	und	danach	die	Turteltäubchen,	und	endlich
in	and	afterwards	the	turtledoves	and	finally

schwirrten	und	schwärmten	alle	Vöglein	unter	dem
whirred	and	swarmed	all	small birds	under	the

Himmel	herein	und	ließen	sich	um	die	Asche	nieder.
sky	in	and	let	self (themselves)	around	the	ashes	down

Und	die	Täubchen	nickten	mit	den	Köpfchen	und
And	the	doves	nodded	with	the	little heads	and

fingen	an	pick,	pick,	pick,	pick,	und	da	fingen	die
started to		pick	pick	pick	pick	and	there	started	the

übrigen	auch	an	pick,	pick,	pick,	pick,	und	lasen	alle
remaining	also	to	pick	pick	pick	pick	and	sorted	all

guten	Körnlein	in	die	Schüssel.	Kaum	war	eine	Stunde
good	little grains	in	the	dish	Hardly	was	one	hour

herum,	so	waren	sie	schon	fertig	und	flogen	alle
around (passed)	so	were	they	already	finished	and	flew	all

wieder	hinaus.	Da	brachte	das	Mädchen	die	Schüssel
again	outside	Then	brought	the	girl	the	dish

der	Stiefmutter,	freute	sich	und	glaubte,	es	dürfte	nun
(to) the	stepmother	was pleased	itself (herself)	and	believed	it (she)	might	now

mit	auf	die	Hochzeit	gehen.
with (join)	to	the	wedding	go

Aber	sie	sprach,	"nein,	Aschenputtel,	du	hast	keine
But	she	spoke	no	Aschenputtel (Cinderella)	you	have	no

Kleider,	und	kannst	nicht	tanzen,	du	wirst	nur
dresses	and	can	not	dance	you	will be	only

ausgelacht."
laughed at

Als	es	nun	weinte,	sprach	sie	"wenn	du	mir	zwei
As	it (she)	now	cried	spoke	she	if	you	me	two

Schüsseln	voll	Linsen	in	einer	Stunde	aus	der	Asche
dishes	full	lentils	in	one	hour	from	the	ashes

rein	lesen	kannst,	so	sollst	du	mitgehen"	und	dachte,
clean	sort	can	so	will	you	go along	and	thought

"das	kann	es	ja	nimmermehr."
that	can	it (she)	yes	never anymore

Als	sie	die	zwei	Schüsseln	Linsen	in	die	Asche
As	she	the	two	dishes	lentils	in	the	ashes

geschüttet	hatte,	ging	das	Mädchen	durch	die	Hintertür
poured	had	went	the	girl	through	the	back door

nach	dem	Garten	und	rief	"ihr	zahmen	Täubchen,	ihr
to	the	garden	and	called	you	tame	doves	you

Turteltäubchen,	all	ihr	Vöglein	unter	dem	Himmel,	kommt
turtledoves	all	you	small birds	under	the	sky	come

und	helft	mit	lesen,
and	help	with	sorting

die	guten	ins	Töpfchen,
the	good	in the	little pot

die	schlechten	ins	Kröpfchen."
the	bad	in the	little pouch (crop)

Da	kamen	zum	Küchenfenster	zwei	weiße	Täubchen
There	came	to the	kitchen window	two	white	little doves

herein	und	danach	die	Turteltäubchen,	und	endlich
in	and	afterwards	the	turtledoves	and	finally

schwirrten	und	schwärmten	alle	Vögel	unter	dem	Himmel
whirred	and	swarmed	all	birds	under	the	sky

herein	und	ließen	sich	um	die	Asche	nieder.
in	and	let	self (themselves)	around	the	ashes	down

Und	die	Täubchen	nickten	mit	ihren	Köpfchen	und
And	the	doves	nodded	with	their	little heads	and

fingen	an	pick,	pick,	pick,	pick,	und	da	fingen	die
started (to)		pick	pick	pick	pick	and	then	started	the

übrigen	auch	an	pick,	pick,	pick,	pick,	und	lasen	alle
remaining	also	(to)	pick	pick	pick	pick	and	sorted	all

guten	Körner	in	die	Schüsseln.	Und	ehe	eine	halbe
good	grains	into	the	dishes	And	before	one	half

Stunde	herum	war,	waren	sie	schon	fertig,	und	flogen
hour	around (passed)	was	were	they	already	finished	and	flew

alle	wieder	hinaus.
all	again	outside

Da	trug	das	Mädchen	die	Schüsseln	zu	der	Stiefmutter,
There	carried	the	Girl	the	dishes	to	the	stepmother

freute	sich	und	glaubte,	nun	dürfte	es	mit	auf	die
was pleased	herself	and	believed	now	might	it (she)	with	to	the

Hochzeit	gehen.	Aber	sie	sprach	"es	hilft	dir	alles
wedding	go	But	she	spoke	it	helps	you	all

nichts,	du	kommst	nicht	mit,	denn	du	hast	keine
not	you	come	not	with	because	you	have	no

Kleider	und	kannst	nicht	tanzen;	wir	müßten	uns	deiner
dresses	and	can	not	dance	we	would have	us	for you

schämen."	Darauf	kehrte	sie	ihm	den	Rücken	zu	und
to be ashamed	Whereupon	turned	she	it (her)	the	back	(to)	and

eilte	mit	ihren	zwei	stolzen	Töchtern	fort.
hurried	with	her	two	proud	daughters	away

Als	nun	niemand	mehr	daheim	war,	ging	Aschenputtel
As	now	nobody	more	at home	was	went	Aschenputtel (Cinderella)

zu	seiner	Mutter	Grab	unter	den	Haselbaum	und	rief:
to	her	mother's	grave	under	the	hazeltree	and	called

"Bäumchen, rüttel dich und schüttel dich,
little tree shake yourself and vibrate (stir) yourself

wirf Gold und Silber über mich."
throw gold and silver over me

Da warf ihm der Vogel ein golden und silbern Kleid
Then threw it (her) the bird a gold and silver dress

herunter und mit Seide und Silber ausgestickte
down and with silk and silver embroidered

Pantoffeln. In aller Eile zog es das Kleid an und
slippers In all haste put it (she) the dress on and

ging zur Hochzeit. Seine Schwestern aber und die
went to the wedding It's (Her) sisters however and the

Stiefmutter kannten es nicht und meinten, es müsse
stepmother knew it not and thought it must

eine fremde Königstochter sein, so schön sah es aus
a foreign king's daughter be so beautiful looked it (she) out

in dem goldenen Kleide. An Aschenputtel dachten sie
in the golden dress Of Aschenputtel (Cinderella) thought they

gar nicht und dachten, es säße daheim im Schmutz
at all not and thought it (she) would sit at home in the dirt

und suchte die Linsen aus der Asche.
and searched the lentils out of the ashes

Der	Königssohn	kam	ihm	entgegen,	nahm	es	bei	der
The	king's son	came	it	against	took	it (her)	by	the

Hand	und	tanzte	mit	ihm.	Er	wollte	auch	sonst	mit
hand	and	danced	with	it (her)	He	wanted	also	otherwise	with

niemand	tanzen,	also	daß	er	ihm	die	Hand	nicht
nobody	dance	thus	that	he	it (her)	the	hand	not

losließ,	und	wenn	ein	anderer	kam,	es	aufzufordern,
released	and	if	an	other one	came	it (her)	to request

sprach	er,	"das	ist	meine	Tänzerin."
spoke	he	that	is	my	dancer (dancepartner)

Es	tanzte,	bis	es	Abend	war,	da	wollte	es	nach
It (She)	danced	until	it	evening	was	then	wanted	it (she)	to

Haus	gehen.	Der	Königssohn	aber	sprach,	"ich
house	go	The	king's son	however	spoke	I

gehe	mit	und	begleite	dich",	denn	er	wollte	sehen,
go with (accompany)		and	escort	you	because	he	wanted	to see

wem	das	schöne	Mädchen	angehörte.
whom	the	beautiful	girl	belonged

Sie	entwischte	ihm	aber	und	sprang	in	das	Taubenhaus.
She	escaped	him	however	and	jumped	in	the	pigeon house

Nun	wartete	der	Königssohn,	bis	der	Vater	kam,	und
Now	waited	the	king's son	until	the	father	came	and

sagte	ihm,	das	fremde	Mädchen	wär	in	das
told	him	the	unknown	girl	was	in	the

Taubenhaus	gesprungen.
pigeon house	jumped

Der	Alte	dachte,	"sollte	es	Aschenputtel	sein?"	und	sie
The	old one	thought	should	it	Aschenputtel (Cinderella)	be	and	they

mußten	ihm	Axt	und	Hacken	bringen,	damit	er	das
had	him	axe	and	pick	to bring	with that	he	the

Taubenhaus	entzweischlagen	konnte,	aber	es	war
pigeon house	smash	could	but	it	was

niemand	darin.
nobody	therein

Und	als	sie	ins	Haus	kamen,	lag	Aschenputtel	in
And	as	they	in the	house	came	lay	Aschenputtel (Cinderella)	in

seinen	schmutzigen	Kleidern	in	der	Asche,	und	ein
its (her)	dirty	dresses	in	the	ashes	and	on

trübes	Öllämpchen	brannte	im	Schornstein:
gloomy	small oil lamp	burned	in the	chimney

denn   Aschenputtel   war   geschwind   aus   dem   Taubenhaus
because   Aschenputtel   was   hastily   out of   the   pigeon house
(Cinderella)

hinten   herabgesprungen,   und   war   zu   dem   Haselbäumchen
in the back   jumped down   and   was   to   the   little hazel tree

gelaufen: da   hatte   es   die   schönen   Kleider   abgezogen
run   there   had   it   the   beautiful   dresses   taken off
(she)

und   aufs   Grab   gelegt   und   der   Vogel   hatte   sie   wieder
and   on the   grave   laid down   and   the   bird   had   them   again

weggenommen,   und   dann   hatte   es   sich   in   seinem
taken away   and   then   had   it   itself   in   its
(she)   (herself)   (her)

grauen   Kittelchen   in   die   Küche   zur   Asche   gesetzt.
grey   little robe   in   the   kitchen   onto   the ashes   set

Am   andern   Tag,   als   das   Fest   von   neuem   anhub,   und
On the   other   day   as   the   feast   of   new   began   and
(next)

die   Eltern   und   Stiefschwestern   wieder   fort   waren,   ging
the   parents   and   stepsisters   again   away   were   went

Aschenputtel   zu   dem   Haselbaum   und   sprach:
Aschenputtel   to   the   hazeltree   and   spoke
(Cinderella)

"Bäumchen,   rüttel   dich   und   schüttel   dich,
Little tree   shake   yourself and   stir   yourself

wirf   Gold   und   Silber   über   mich."
throw   gold   and   silver   over   me

Da   warf   der   Vogel   ein   noch   viel   stolzeres   Kleid   herab
Then   threw   the   bird   one   still   much   more majestic   dress   down

als   am   vorigen   Tag.   Und   als   es   mit   diesem   Kleide
as   on the   previous   day   And   as   it   with   this   dress
                                                (she)

auf   der   Hochzeit   erschien,   erstaunte   jedermann   über
at   the   wedding   appeared   wondered   everyone   at

seine   Schönheit.
its   beauty
(her)

Der   Königssohn   aber   hatte   gewartet,   bis   es   kam,   nahm
The   king's son   however   had   waited   until   it   came,   took
                                                (she)

es   gleich   bei   der   Hand   und   tanzte   nur   allein   mit
it   immediately by   the   hand   and   danced   just   only   with
(her)

ihm.   Wenn   die   andern   kamen   und   es   aufforderten,
it   If   the   others   came   and   it   requested
(her)   (her)

sprach   er   "das   ist   meine   Tänzerin."
spoke   he   that   is   my   dancer
                              (dancing partner)

Als	es	nun	Abend	war,	wollte	es	fort	und	der
As	it	now	evening	was	wanted	it (she)	(to go) away	and	the

Königssohn	ging	ihm	nach	und	wollte	sehen,	in
king's son	went	it (her)	after	and	wanted	to see	in

welches	Haus	es	ging:	aber	es	sprang	ihm	fort	und
which	house	it (she)	went	but	it (she)	leapt (from)	him	away	and

in	den	Garten	hinter	dem	Haus.	Darin	stand	ein
into	the	garden	behind	the	house	Therein	stood	a

schöner	großer	Baum,	an	dem	die	herrlichsten	Birnen
beautiful	large	tree	from	which	the	most delicious	pears

hingen,	es	kletterte	so	behend	wie	ein	Eichhörnchen
hung	it (she)	climbed	so	swiftly	as	a	squirrel

zwischen	die	Äste,	und	der	Königssohn	wußte	nicht,
between	the	branches	and	the	king's son	knew	not

wo	es	hingekommen	war.
where	it (she)	gotten to	was

Er	wartete	aber,	bis	der	Vater	kam,	und	sprach	zu
He	waited	however	until	the	father	arrived	and	spoke	to

ihm	"das	fremde	Mädchen	ist	mir	entwischt,	und	ich
him	the	unknown	girl	is	from me	escaped	and	I

glaube,	es	ist	auf	den	Birnbaum	gesprungen."
believe	it (she)	is	up into	the	pear tree	jumped

Der	Vater	dachte	"sollte	es	Aschenputtel	sein?"	ließ
The	father	thought	would	it	Aschenputtel (Cinderella)	be	let

sich	die	Axt	holen	und	hieb	den	Baum	um,	aber	es
himself	the	axe	get	and	chopped	the	tree	down	but	it

war	niemand	darauf.	Und	als	sie	in	die	Küche	kamen,
was	nobody	thereon (therein)	And	as	they	in	the	kitchen	came

lag	Aschenputtel	da	in	der	Asche,	wie	sonst	auch,
laid	Aschenputtel	there	in	the	ashes	as	otherwise (always)	also

denn	es	war	auf	der	andern	Seite	vom	Baum
because	it (she)	was	on	the	other	side	of the	tree

herabgesprungen,	hatte	dem	Vogel	auf	dem
jumped down	had	the	bird	in	the

Haselbäumchen	die	schönen	Kleider	wiedergebracht	und
hazel tree	the	beautiful	dresses	returned	and

sein	graues	Kittelchen	angezogen.
its (her)	grey	little robe	put on

Am	dritten	Tag,	als	die	Eltern	und	Schwestern	fort
On the	third	day	as	the	parents	and	sisters	away

waren,	ging	Aschenputtel	wieder	zu	seiner	Mutter	Grab
were	went	Aschenputtel (Cinderella)	again	to	her	mother's	grave

und	sprach	zu	dem	Bäumchen:
and	spoke	to	the	little tree

"Bäumchen, rüttel dich und schüttel dich,
Little tree   shake   yourself and stir   yourself

wirf Gold und Silber über mich."
throw gold and silver over me

Nun warf ihm der Vogel ein Kleid herab, das war so
Now threw it the bird a dress down that was so
     (her)

prächtig und glänzend, wie es noch keins gehabt hatte,
magnificent and shining as it yet none had had
                    (she)

und die Pantoffeln waren ganz golden. Als es in dem
und the slippers were completely of gold As it in the
                                       (she)

Kleid zu der Hochzeit kam, wußten sie alle nicht, was
dress to the wedding came knew they all not what

sie vor Verwunderung sagen sollten. Der Königssohn
they of amazement say should The king's son

tanzte ganz allein mit ihm, und wenn es einer
danced completely only with it and if it one
                          (her)   (her)

aufforderte, sprach er "das ist meine Tänzerin."
requested spoke he that is my dancer
                                 (dancepartner)

Als es nun Abend war, wollte Aschenputtel fort, und
As it now evening was wanted Aschenputtel (to go) away and
(Cinderella)

der Königssohn wollte es begleiten, aber es entsprang
he king's son wanted it to accompany but it leapt from
(her) (she)

hm so geschwind, daß er nicht folgen konnte. Der
im so swiftly that he not follow could The

Königssohn hatte aber eine List gebraucht, und hatte
king's son had however a trick used and had

die ganze Treppe mit Pech bestreichen lassen: da war,
he whole stairs with pitch coated let then was

als es hinabsprang, der linke Pantoffel des Mädchens
s it jumped down the left slipper of the girl
(she)

hängen geblieben. Der Königssohn hob ihn auf, und er
ang remained The king's son lifted it up and it

war klein und zierlich und ganz golden. Am nächsten
vas small and delicate and completely of gold On the next

Morgen ging er damit zu dem Mann und sagte zu
morning went he with it to the man and said to

hm "keine andere soll meine Gemahlin werden als die,
im none other shall my wife become as the one

an deren Fuß dieser goldene Schuh paßt."
n whose foot this golden shoe fits

Da	freuten	sich	die	beiden	Schwestern,	denn	sie	hatten
then	were pleased	themselves	the	both	sisters	because	they	had

schöne	Füße.	Die	älteste	ging	mit	dem	Schuh	in	die
beautiful	feet	The	oldest	went	with	the	shoe	in	the

Kammer	und	wollte	ihn	anprobieren,	und	die	Mutter
chamber	and	wanted	it	try on	and	the	mother

stand	dabei.	Aber	sie	konnte	mit	der	großen	Zehe
stood	by	But	it	could	with	the	large	toe

nicht	hineinkommen,	und	der	Schuh	war	ihr	zu	klein,
not	come in	and	the	shoe	was	to her	too	small

da	reichte	ihr	die	Mutter	ein	Messer	und	sprach	"hau
there	reached (handed)	to her	the	mother	a	knife	and	spoke	chop

die	Zehe	ab:	wann	du	Königin	bist,	so	brauchst	du
the	toe	off	when	you	Queen	are	so	need	you

nicht	mehr	zu	Fuß	zu	gehen."	Das	Mädchen	hieb	die
not	more	on	foot	to	go	The	girl	chopped	the

Zehe	ab,	zwängte	den	Fuß	in	den	Schuh,	verbiß	den
toe	off	squeezed	the	foot	into	the	shoe	suppressed	the

Schmerz	und	ging	heraus	zum	Königssohn.	Da	nahm
pain	and	went	out	to the	king's son	There	took

er	sie	als	seine	Braut	aufs	Pferd	und	ritt	mit	ihr	fort.
he	her	as	his	bride	on the	horse	and	rode	with	her	away

Sie mußten aber an dem Grabe vorbei, da saßen die
They had however by the grave past there sat the

zwei Täubchen auf dem Haselbäumchen und riefen
two little doves on the hazel tree and called
(up in)

"rucke di guck, rucke di guck,
rucke di guck   rucke di guck
(german dove language)

Blut ist im Schuck (Schuh) :
Blood is in the Schuck Shoe
(dove language for shoe)

Der Schuck ist zu klein,
The Schuck is too small
(shoe)

die rechte Braut sitzt noch daheim."
the right bride sits still at home
(real)

Da blickte er auf ihren Fuß und sah, wie das Blut
There looked he at her foot and saw how the blood

herausquoll. Er wendete sein Pferd um, brachte die
poured out He turned his Horse around brought the

falsche Braut wieder nach Hause und sagte, das wäre
wrong bride back to house and said that was

nicht die rechte, die andere Schwester solle den Schuh
not the right one the other sister should the shoe

anziehen.
put on

Da	ging	diese	in	die	Kammer	und	kam	mit	den
There	went	this one	in	the	chamber	and	came	with	the

Zehen	glücklich	in	den	Schuh,	aber	die	Ferse	war	zu
toes	fortunately	in	the	shoe	but	the	heel	was	too

groß.	Da	reichte	ihr	die	Mutter	ein	Messer	und	sprach
big	There (Then)	handed	her	the	mother	a	knife	and	said

"hau	ein	Stück	von	der	Ferse	ab:	wann	du	Königin
chop	a	piece	of	the	heel	off	when	you	queen

bist,	brauchst	du	nicht	mehr	zu	Fuß	zu	gehen."
are	need	you	not	anymore	on	foot	to	go

Das	Mädchen	hieb	ein	Stück	von	der	Ferse	ab,
The	girl	chopped	a	piece	of	the	heel	off

zwängte	den	Fuß	in	den	Schuh,	verbiß	den	Schmerz
squeezed	the	foot	in	the	shoe	suppressed	the	pain

und	ging	heraus	zum	Königssohn.	Da	nahm	er	sie
and	went	out	to	king's son	There	took	he	her

als	seine	Braut	aufs	Pferd	und	ritt	mit	ihr	fort.	Als
as	his	bride	on the	horse	and	rode	with	her	away	As

sie	an	dem	Haselbäumchen	vorbeikamen,	saßen	die
she	by	the	hazel tree	went past	sat	the

zwei	Täubchen	darauf	und	riefen:
two	little doves	thereupon	and	called

"rucke di guck, rucke di guck,
rucke di guck   rucke di guck
(translates roughly to cucurucu)

Blut ist im Schuck (Schuh):
Blood is in the schuck shoe
                  (free rhyme for shoe)

Der Schuck ist zu klein,
the schuck is too small
  (shoe)

die rechte Braut sitzt noch daheim."
the right bride sits still at home

Er blickte nieder auf ihren Fuß und sah, wie das
He looked down on her foot and saw how the

Blut aus dem Schuh quoll und an den weißen
blood out of the shoe poured and on the white

Strümpfen ganz rot heraufgestiegen war.
socks completely red risen was

Da wendete er sein Pferd und brachte die falsche
There turned he his horse and brought the wrong

Braut wieder nach Haus. "Das ist auch nicht die
bride back home That is also not the

rechte," sprach er, "habt ihr keine andere Tochter?"
right one spoke he have you no other daughters

"Nein" sagte der Mann, nur von meiner verstorbenen
No said the man only of my deceased

Frau ist noch ein kleines schmutziges Aschenputtel da:
wife is still a small dirty Aschenputtel there
(Cinderella) (but)

das kann unmöglich die Braut sein. " Der Königssohn
that can not possibly the bride be The king's son

sprach, er sollte es heraufschicken, die Mutter aber
spoke he should it send up the mother however
(her)

antwortete" ach nein, das ist viel zu schmutzig, das
answered oh no it is much too dirty that

darf sich nicht sehen lassen. " Er wollte es aber
may itself not let see He wanted it however
(show) (her)

durchaus haben, und Aschenputtel mußte gerufen werden.
totally have and Aschenputtel had called to be
(Cinderella)

Da wusch es sich erst Hände und Angesicht rein,
Then washed it itself first hands and face clean
(she) (herself)

ging dann hin und neigte sich vor dem Königssohn,
went then there and bowed herself for the king's son

der ihm den goldenen Schuh reichte.
that it the golden shoe reached
(her) (handed)

Dann setzte es sich auf einen Schemel, zog den Fuß
Then set it itself on a stool pulled the foot
(she) (herself)

aus dem schweren Holzschuh und steckte ihn in den
out of the heavy wooden shoe and put it in the

Pantoffel, der war wie angegossen. Und als es sich
slipper it was as if cast on And as it itself
(fit perfectly) (she) (herself)

in die Höhe richtete und der König ihm ins Gesicht
in the height erected and the king it in the face
(raised) (her)

sah, so erkannte er das schöne Mädchen, das mit
saw so recognized he the beautiful girl that with

ihm getanzt hatte, und rief "das ist die rechte Braut."
him danced had and called that is the right bride

Die Stiefmutter und die beiden Schwestern erschraken
The stepmother and the both sisters became frightened

und wurden bleich vor Arger: er aber nahm
and became white of bad he however took

Aschenputtel aufs Pferd und ritt mit ihm fort. Als sie
Aschenputtel on the horse and rode with it away As they
(Cinderella) (her)

an dem Haselbäumchen vorbeikamen, riefen die zwei
by the hazel tree went past called the two

weißen Täubchen:
white doves

"rucke di guck,   rucke di guck
rucke di guck   rucke di guck

kein   Blut   im   Schuck
no   blood   in   schuck
                     (shoe)

Der   Schuck   ist   nicht   zu   klein,
The   schuck   is   not   too   small
      (shoe)

die   rechte   Braut,   die   führt   er   heim."
the   right   bride   that   leads   he   home

Und   als   sie   das   gerufen   hatten,   kamen   sie   beide
And   as   they   that   called   had   came   they   both

herabgeflogen   und   setzten   sich   dem   Aschenputtel   auf
down down   and   set   themselves   the   Aschenputtel   on
                                            (Cinderella)

die   Schultern,   eine   rechts,   die   andere   links,   und
the   shoulders   one   on the right   the   other one   on the left   and

blieben   da   sitzen.   Als   die   Hochzeit   mit   dem
remained   there   sit   As   the   wedding   with   the

Königssohn   sollte   gehalten   werden,   kamen   die   falschen
king's son   should   held   be   came   the   false

Schwestern,   wollten   sich   einschmeicheln   und   teil   an
sisters   wanted   themselves   wheedle in   and   part   on

seinem   Glück   nehmen.
her   fortune   take

Als die Brautleute nun zur Kirche gingen, war die
As the bride people now to church went was the

älteste zur rechten, die jüngste zur linken Seite: da
oldest to the right the youngest to the left side there

pickten die Tauben einer jeden das eine Auge aus.
picked the doves one both the one eye out

Hernach, als sie herausgingen, war die älteste zur
Afterwards as they went out was the oldest to the

linken und die jüngste zur rechten: da pickten die
left and the youngest to the right there picked the

Tauben einer jeden das andere Auge aus. Und waren
doves one both the other eye out And were

sie also für ihre Bosheit und Falschheit mit Blindheit
they thus for their malice and falsehood with blindness

auf ihr Lebtag bestraft.
for their liveday punished
(the rest of their lives)

49   Aschenputtel

BRÜDERCHEN UND SCHWESTERCHEN
LITTLE BROTHER AND LITTLE SISTER

Brüderchen	nahm	sein	Schwesterchen	an	der	Hand	und
Little brother	took	his	little sister	by	the	hand	and

sprach:	"Seit	die	Mutter	tot	ist,	haben	wir	keine	gute
said	Since	the	mother	dead	is	have	we	no	good

Stunde	mehr;	die	Stiefmutter	schlägt	uns	alle	Tage	und
hour	anymore	the	stepmother	beats	us	all	days	and

stößt	uns	mit	den	Füßen	fort.	Die	harten	Brotkrusten,
kicks	us	with	the	feet	away	The	hard	bread crusts

die	übrigbleiben,	sind	unsere	Speise,	und	dem
that	remain	are	our	meal	and	the

Hündchen	unter	dem	Tisch	geht's	besser,	dem	wirft	sie
little dog	under	the	table	fares it	better	it	throws	she

doch	manchmal	einen	guten	Bissen	zu.	Daß	Gott
still	sometimes	a	good	bite	to	That	God

erbarm,	wenn	das	unsere	Mutter	wüßte!	Komm,	wir
pities	if	that	our	mother	would know	Come	we

wollen	miteinander	in	die	weite	Welt	gehen."
should	with eachother	in	the	wide	world	go

Sie	gingen	den	ganzen	Tag,	und	wenn	es	regnete,
They	went	the	whole	day	and	if	it	rained

sprach	das	Schwesterlein:	"Gott	und	unsere	Herzen,	die
said1	the	little sister	God	and	our	hearts	they

weinen	zusammen!"
cry	together

Abends	kamen	sie	in	einen	großen	Wald	und	waren
In the evening	came	they	in	a	large	forest	and	were

so	müde	von	Jammer,	vom	Hunger	und	von	dem
o	tired	of the	misery	of the	hunger	and	of	the

angen	Weg,	daß	sie	sich	in	einen	hohlen	Baum
ong	road	that	they	themselves	in	a	hollow	tree

setzten	und	einschliefen.
et	and	fell asleep

Am	andern	Morgen,	als	sie	aufwachten,	stand	die
In the	other (next)	morning	as	they	woke up	stood	the

Sonne	schon	hoch	am	Himmel	und	schien	heiß	in
un	already	high	in the	sky	and	shone	hot	in

den	Baum	hinein.
he	tree	inside

Da	sprach	das	Brüderchen:	"Schwesterchen,	mich	dürstet,
There	spoke	the	little brother	Little sister	me it thirsts (I am thirsty)	

wenn	ich	ein	Brünnlein	wüßte,	ich	ging'	und	tränk'
if	I	a	little spring	would know	I	went	and	would drink

einmal;	ich	meine,	ich	hört'	eins	rauschen."
a bit	I	think	I	hear	a	murmur (of water)

Brüderchen	stand	auf,	nahm	Schwesterchen	an	der
Little brother	stood	up	took	little sister	by	the

Hand,	und	sie	wollten	das	Brünnlein	suchen.	Die	böse
hand	and	they	wished	the	little spring	to search	The	evil

Stiefmutter	aber	war	eine	Hexe	und	hatte	wohl
stepmother	however	was	a	witch	and	had	certainly

gesehen,	wie	die	beiden	Kinder	fortgegangen	waren,	war
seen	how	the	both	children	away gone (went off)	were	was

ihnen	nachgeschlichen,	heimlich,	wie	die	Hexen
them	after crept (crept after)	secretly	as	the	witches

schleichen,	und	hatte	alle	Brunnen	im	Walde	verwünscht.
creep	and	had	every	well	in the	forest	cursed

Als sie nun ein Brünnlein fanden, das so glitzerig
As they now a little well found that so glittering

über die Steine sprang, wollte das Brüderchen daraus
over the stones jumped wanted the little brother off it

trinken; aber das Schwesterchen hörte, wie es im
drink but the little sister heard how it in

Rauschen sprach:
murmuring spoke

"Wer aus mir trinkt, wird ein Tiger,
Who from me drinks becomes a tiger

wer aus mir trinkt, wird ein Tiger."
who from me drinks becomes a tiger

Da rief das Schwesterchen:
Then called the little sister

"Ich bitte dich, Brüderchen, trink nicht, sonst wirst du
I beg you little brother drink not otherwise become you

ein wildes Tier und zerreißt mich."
a wild animal and tear up me

Das	Brüderchen	trank	nicht,	obgleich	es	so	großen
The	little brother	drank	not	although	it (he)	so	much

Durst	hatte,	und	sprach:	"Ich	will	warten	bis	zur
thirst	had	and	spoke	I	shall	wait	(to)	until the

nächsten	Quelle."
next	well

Als	sie	zum	zweiten	Brünnlein	kamen,	hörte	das
As	they	to the	second	little spring	came	heard	the

Schwesterchen,	wie	auch	dieses	sprach:
little sister	how	also	this one	spoke

"Wer	aus	mir	trinkt,	wird	ein	Wolf,
Who	from	me	drinks	becomes	a	wolf

wer	aus	mir	trinkt,	wird	ein	Wolf."
who	from	me	drinks	becomes	a	wolf

Da	rief	das	Schwesterchen"Brüderchen,	ich	bitte	dich,
Then	called	the	little sister Little brother	I	ask	you

trink	nicht,	sonst	wirst	du	ein	Wolf	und	frissest	mich."
drink	not	otherwise	become	you	a	wolf	and	eat	me

Das Brüderchen trank nicht und sprach: "Ich will
The little brother drank not and spoke I shall

warten, bis wir zur nächsten Quelle kommen, aber
wait until we onto the next well come but

dann muß ich trinken, du magst sagen, was du willst;
then must I drink you may say what you want

nein Durst ist gar zu groß."
nay thirst is quite too great
(much)

Und als sie zum dritten Brünnlein kamen, hörte das
And as they to the third little well came heard the

Schwesterlein, wie es im Rauschen sprach:
little sister as it in murmurs spoke

Wer aus mir trinkt, wird ein Reh,
Who from me drinks becomes a deer

wer aus mir trinkt, wird ein Reh."
who from me drinks becomes a deer

Das Schwesterchen sprach: "Ach, Brüderchen, trink nicht,
The little sister spoke Oh little brother drink not

sonst wirst du ein Reh und läufst mir fort."
otherwise become you a deer and run from me away

Aber das Brüderchen hatte sich gleich beim Brünnlein
ut the little brother had himself directly by the well

niedergekniet, und von dem Wasser getrunken, und wie
neeled down and from the water drunk and as

die ersten Tropfen auf seine Lippen gekommen waren,
ne first drops on his lips come were

ag es da als ein Rehkälbchen. Nun weinte das
ty it there as a deer calf Now cried the
(he)

Schwesterchen über das arme verwünschte Brüderchen,
ttle sister over the poor cursed little brother

und das Rehchen weinte auch und Saß so traurig
nd the little deer cried also and sat so sadly

neben ihm. Da sprach das Mädchen endlich: "Sei still,
eside it Then spoke the girl finally Be quiet
(her)

ebes Rehchen, ich will dich ja nimmermehr verlassen."
ear little deer I shall you yes never more leave

Dann band es sein goldenes Strumpfband ab und tat
hen bound it its golden sock band off and did
(she) (her)

s dem Rehchen um den Hals und rupfte Binsen und
the little deer around the neck and plucked bulrushes and

ocht ein weiches Seil daraus.
ove a soft rope from it

Daran band es das Tierchen und führte es weiter und
To it bound it the little animal and led it further and
(she)

ging immer tiefer in den Wald hinein.
went still deeper into the Forest inside

Und als sie lange, lange gegangen waren, kamen sie
And as they long long gone were came they

endlich an ein kleines Haus, und das Mädchen schaute
finally onto a small house and the girl looked

hinein, und weil es leer war, dachte es: "Hier können
inside and because it empty was thought it Here can
(she)

wir bleiben und wohnen." Da suchte es dem Rehchen
we remain and live There searched it the little deer
(she)

Laub und Moos zu einem weichen Lager, und jeden
leaves and moss for a soft lair and every

Morgen ging es aus und sammelte Wurzeln, Beeren
morning went it off and collected roots berries

und Nüsse, und für das Rehchen brachte es zartes
and nuts and for the little deer brought it tender
(she)

Gras mit, war vergnügt und spielte vor ihm herum.
grass with was happy and played with him around

Abends,	wenn	Schwesterchen	müde	war	und	sein	Gebet
In the evening	if	little sister	tired	was	and	its (her)	prayer

gesagt	hatte,	legte	es	seinen	Kopf	auf	den	Rücken
said	had	put	it (she)	its (her)	head	onto	the	back

des	Rehkälbchens,	das	war	sein	Kissen,	darauf	es
of the	deer calf	that	was	its (her)	pillow	whereupon	it (she)

sanft	einschlief.	Und	hätte	das	Brüderchen	nur	seine
softly	fell asleep	And	would have	the	little brother	only	his

menschliche	Gestalt	gehabt,	es	wäre	ein	herrliches
human	shape	had	it	would be	a	wonderful

Leben	gewesen.	Das	dauerte	eine	Zeitlang,	daß	sie	so
life	been	That	lasted	a	while	that	they	so

allein	in	der	Wildnis	waren.	Auf	einen	Tag	aber
alone	in	the	wilderness	were	On	one	day	however

trug	es sich	zu,	daß	der	König	des	Landes	eine	große
carried itself on (it happened)			that	the	king	of the	land	a	large

Jagd	in	dem	Wald	hielt.	Da	schallte	das	Hörnerblasen,
hunt	in	the	forest	held	There	sounded	the	horn blowing

Hundegebell	und	das	lustige	Geschrei	der	Jäger	durch
dog barks	and	the	merry	shouting	of the	hunters	through

die	Bäume,	und	das	Rehlein	hörte	es	und	wäre	gar
the	trees	and	the	little deer	heard	it	and	would be (would have)	quite

zu	gerne	dabeigewesen.
too	eagerly	participated

"Ach",   sprach   es   zum   Schwesterlein,   "laß   mich   hinaus
Oh   spoke   it   to the little sister   leave   me   outside

in   die   Jagd,   ich   kann's   nicht   länger   mehr   aushalten",
in   the   hunt   I   can it   no   longer   anymore   bear

und   bat   so   lange,   bis   es   einwilligte.   "Aber",   sprach   es
and   asked   so   long   until   it   consented   But   spoke   it
                                         (she)   (she)

zu   ihm,   "komm   mir   ja   abends   wieder,   vor   den   wilden
to   him   come   to me   yes   in the evening again   for   the   wild

Jägern   schließ'   ich   mein   Türlein;   und   damit   ich   dich
hunters   close   I   my   little door   and   with that   I   you
                                                             (so)

kenne,   so   klopf   und   sprich: 'Mein   Schwesterlein,   laß
know , recognize   so   knock   and   speak   my   little sister   let

mich   herein!'   Und   wenn   du   nicht   so   sprichst,   so
me   in here   And   if   you   not   thus   speak   so

schließ   ich   mein   Türlein   nicht   auf."
close   I   my   little door   not   open , un-
aufschließen; unlock)   (aufschließen; unlock)

Nun   sprang   das   Rehchen   hinaus   und   es   war   ihm   so
Now   jumped   the   little deer   outside   and   it   was   to him   so

wohl   und   es   war   so   lustig   in   freier   Luft.
good   and   it   was   so   merry   in   the free   air
               (he)

Der	König	und	seine	Jäger	sahen	das	schöne	Tier
The	king	and	his	hunters	saw	the	beautiful	animal

und	setzten	ihm	nach,	aber	sie	konnten	es	nicht
and	set	it	after	but	they	could	it	not
	(nachsetzen; chase)		(nachsetzen; chase)					

einholen,	und	wenn	sie	meinten,	sie	hätten	es	gewiß,
overtake	and	when	they	thought	they	had	it	certainly

da	sprang	es	über	das	Gebüsch	weg	und	war
there	jumped	it	over	the	bushes	away	and	was

verschwunden.
gone

Als	es	dunkel	ward,	lief	es	zu	dem	Häuschen,	klopfte
As	it	dark	became	ran	it	to	the	little house	knocked

und	sprach:	"Mein	Schwesterlein,	laß	mich	herein."
and	spoke	My	little sister	let	me	in here

Da	ward	ihm	die	kleine	Tür	aufgetan,	es	sprang
There	was	to him	the	small	door	opened	it	jumped

hinein	und	ruhete	sich	die	ganze	Nacht	auf	seinem
inside	and	rested	itself	the	whole	night	on	its
		(ausruhen; to rest)						

weichen	Lager	aus.
soft	bed	(ausruhen; to rest)

Am	andern	Morgen	ging	die	Jagd	von	neuem	an,	und
On the	other (next)	morning	went	the	hunt	of new (anew)		on	and

als	das	Rehlein	wieder	das	Hifthorn	hörte	und	das
as	the	little deer	again	the	hunters horn	heard	and	the

"Ho	ho!"	der	Jäger,	da	hatte	es	keine	Ruhe	und
Ho	ho	of the	hunters	then	had	it	no	peace	and

sprach:	"Schwesterchen,	mach	mir	auf,	ich	muß	hinaus."
spoke	little sister	Make	me	open (the door)	I	must	outside (go)

Das	Schwesterchen	öffnete	ihm	die	Tür	und	sprach:
The	little sister	opened	for him	the	door	and	spoke

"Aber	zu	Abend	mußt	du	wieder	da	sein	und	dein
But	in the	evening	must	you	again	there (here)	be	and	your

Sprüchlein	sagen."
little speech	say

Als	der	König	und	seine	Jäger	das	Rehlein	mit	dem
As	the	king	and	his	hunters	the	little deer	with	the

goldenen	Halsband	wiedersahen,	jagten	sie	ihm	alle
golden	collar	saw again	chased	they	it	all

nach,	aber	es	war	ihnen	zu	schnell	und	behend.
after	but	it	was	them	too	fast	and	swift

Das währte den ganzen Tag, endlich aber hatten es
That lasted the whole day finally but had it

die Jäger abends umzingelt, und einer verwundete es
the hunters in the evening encircled and one wounded it

ein wenig am Fuß, so daß es hinken mußte und
a little to the foot so that it limp had to and

langsam fortlief.
slowly ran away

Da schlich ihm ein Jäger nach bis zu dem Häuschen
There sneaked him one hunter after to the little house

und hörte, wie es rief: "Mein Schwesterlein, laß mich
and heard as it called My little sister let me

herein" , und sah, daß die Tür ihm aufgetan und
in here and saw that the door for him opened and

alsbald wieder zugeschlossen ward. Der Jäger ging zum
immediately again locked became The hunter went to the

König und erzählte ihm, was er gesehen und gehört
king and told him what he seen and heard

hatte. Da sprach der König: "Morgen soll noch einmal
had There spoke the king Tomorrow shall yet once more

gejagt werden."
hunted become

Das	Schwesterchen	aber	erschrak	gewaltig,	als	es	sah,
The	little sister	however	frightened	enormously	as	it (she)	saw

daß	sein	Rehkälbchen	verwundet	war.	Es	wusch	ihm
that	its (her)	little deer calf	wounded	was	It (she)	washed	it

das	Blut	ab,	legte	Kräuter	auf	und	sprach:	"Geh	auf
the	blood	off	put	herbs	on	and	spoke	Go	on

dein	Lager,	lieb	Rehchen,	daß	du	wieder	heil	wirst."
your	bed	dear	little deer	that	you	again	well	become

Die	Wunde	aber	war	so	gering,	daß	das	Rehchen	am
The	wound	however	was	so	small	that	the	little deer	on the

Morgen	nichts	mehr	davon	spürte.	Und	als	es	die
morning	nothing	more	of it	felt	And	as	it	the

Jagdlust	wieder	draußen	hörte,	sprach	es:	"Ich	kann's
hunting fun	again	outside	heard	spoke	it	I	can

nicht	aushalten,	ich	muß	dabeisein!"
not	bear (it)	I	must	participate

Das	Schwesterchen	weinte	und	sprach:	"Nun	werden	sie
The	little sister	cried	and	spoke	Now	shall	they

dich	töten,	und	ich	bin	hier	allein	im	Wald	und	bin
you	kill	and	I	am	here	alone	in the	forest	and	am

verlassen	von	aller	Welt,	ich	lass'	dich	nicht	hinaus."
left	of	the whole	world	I	leave	you	not	outside

"So	sterb	'ich	dir	hier	vor	Betrübnis",	antwortete	das
So	die	I	to you	here	of	sadness	answered	the

Rehchen,	"wenn	ich	das	Hifthorn	höre,	so	mein'	ich,
little deer	when	I	the	hunter's horn	hear	so	think	I

ich	müßt'	aus	den	Schuhen	springen!"
I	must	out of	the	shoes	jump

(Aus den Schuhen springen; run off and have fun)

Da	konnte	das	Schwesterchen	nicht	anders	und	schloß
Then	could	the	little sister	not	else	and	closed
					(do anything else)		(aufschließen; op

hm	mit	schwerem	Herzen	die	Tür	auf,	und	das
o him	with	heavy	heart	the	door	open , un-	and	the
						(aufschließen; open)		

Rehchen	sprang	gesund	und	fröhlich	in	den	Wald.	Als
little deer	jumped	healthy	and	merrily	into	the	forest	As

es	der	König	erblickte,	sprach	er	zu	seinen	Jägern:
the	king	saw	spoke	he	to	his	hunters	

Nun	jagt	ihm	nach	den	ganzen	Tag	bis	in	die
Now	chase	it	after	the	whole	day	until	in	the

Nacht,	aber	daß	ihm	keiner	etwas	zuleide	tut."
ight	but	that	it	no one	some	harm	does
					(any)		

Sobald die Sonne untergegangen war, sprach der König
As soon as the sun gone down was spoke the king

zum Jäger: "Nun komm und zeige mir das
to the hunter Now come and show me the

Waldhäuschen." Und als er vor dem Türlein war,
little forest house And as he before the little door was

klopfte er an und rief: "Lieb Schwesterlein, laß mich
knocked he on and called Dear little sister let me
(it)

herein."
in here

Da ging die Tür auf, und der König trat herein, und
There went the door open and the king stepped in here and
(in)

da stand ein Mädchen, das war so schön, wie er
there stood a girl that was so beautiful as he

noch keines gesehen hatte. Das Mädchen erschrak, als
yet none seen had The girl frightened as

es sah, daß ein Mann hereinkam, der eine goldene
it saw that a man came in that a golden
(she)

Krone auf dem Haupt hatte.
crown on the head had

Aber der König sah es freundlich an, reichte ihm die
But the king looked it (her) friendly at reached out it (her) the

Hand und sprach: "Willst du mit mir gehen auf mein
hand and spoke Want you with me go up my

Schloß und meine liebe Frau sein?"
castle and my beloved wife be

"Ach ja", antwortete das Mädchen, "aber das Rehchen
Oh yes answered the girl but the little deer

muß auch mit, das verlass' ich nicht."
must also with (join) that leave I not

Sprach der König: "Es soll bei dir bleiben, solange du
Spoke the king It shall with you remain so long you

lebst, und es soll ihm an nichts fehlen." Indem kam
live and it shall him in nothing lack By then came

es hereingesprungen; da band es das Schwesterchen
it jumped in there bound it the little sister

wieder an das Binsenseil, nahm es selbst in die Hand
again on the bulrush rope took it self in the hand

und ging mit ihm aus dem Waldhäuschen fort.
and went with it out of the little forest house away

Der	König	nahm	das	schöne	Mädchen	auf	sein	Pferd
The	king	took	the	beautiful	girl	up on	his	horse

und	führte	es	in	sein	Schloß,	wo	die	Hochzeit	mit
and	led	it	into	his	castle	where	the	wedding	with

großer	Pracht	gefeiert	wurde,	und	es	war	nun	die
much	splendour	celebrated	became	and	it (she)	was	now	the

Frau	Königin,	und	sie	lebten	lange	Zeit	vergnügt
wife	queen	and	they	lived	long	time	happy

zusammen;	das	Rehlein	ward	gehegt	und	gepflegt	und
together	the	little deer	became	cherished	and	cared for	and

sprang	in	dem	Schloßgarten	herum.
leapt	in	the	palace garden	around

Die	böse	Stiefmutter	aber,	um	derentwillen	die	Kinder
The	evil	stepmother	however	by	whose doing	the	children

in	die	Welt	hineingegangen	waren,	die	meinte	nicht
in	the	world	gone in	were	that one (she)	thought	nothing

anders	als,	Schwesterchen	wäre	von	den	wilden	Tieren
else	as (that)	little sister	would have been	by	the	wild	animals

im	Walde	zerrissen	worden	und	Brüderchen	als	ein
in the	forest	torn up	became	and	little brother	as	a

Rehkalb	von	den	Jägern	totgeschossen.
deer calf	by	the	hunters	shot dead

Als	sie	nun	hörte,	daß	sie	so	glücklich	waren	und
As	she	now	heard	that	they	so	happy	were	and

es	ihnen	so	wohlging,	da	wurden	Neid	und	Mißgunst
them		so	well went	there	became	envy	and	resent

in	ihrem	Herzen	rege	und	ließen	ihr	keine	Ruhe,	wie
	her	heart	stirring	and	left	her	no	peace	how

sie	die	beiden	doch	noch	ins	Unglück	bringen	könnte.
he (them)	those	both	nevertheless	still	in	misfortune	bring	could

Ihre	rechte	Tochter,	die	häßlich	war	wie	die	Nacht
Her	right (real, own)	daughter	that	ugly	was	as	the	night

und	nur	ein	Auge	hatte,	die	machte	ihr	Vorwürfe	und
and	only	one	eye	had	that (she)	made	her	reproaches	and

sprach:	Eine	Königin	zu	werden,	das	Glück	hätte	mir
spoke	A	queen	to	become	that	fortune	would have	to me

gebührt.	"
been entitled	

Sei	nur	still",	sagte	die	Alte	und	sprach	sie	zufrieden,
Be	just	quiet	said	the	old one	and	spoke	she	content

wenn's	Zeit	ist,	will	ich	schon	bei	der	Hand	sein."
when it	time	is	shall	I	already	by	the	hand	be

Als nun die Zeit herangerückt war und die Königin ein
As now the time moved close was and the queen a

schönes Knäblein zur Welt gebracht hatte und der
beautiful little boy into the world born had and the

König gerade auf der Jagd war, nahm die alte Hexe
king just on the hunt was took the old witch

die Gestalt der Kammerfrau an, trat in die Stube, wo
the shape of the chamber woman (on) stepped in the room where

die Königin lag, und sprach zu der Kranken:
the queen lay and spoke to the ill one
(patient)

"Kommt, das Bad ist fertig, das wird Euch wohltun
Come the bath is ready that will you do good

und frische Kräfte geben; geschwind, eh' es kalt wird."
and fresh energy give quikly before it cold becomes

Ihre Tochter war auch bei der Hand, sie trugen die
Her daughter was also at (the) hand they carried the

schwache Königin in die Badstube und legten sie in
weak queen in the bath room and put her in

die Wanne.
the Tub

)ann	schlossen	sie	die	Türe	ab	und	liefen	davon.	In
hen	closed	they	the	door	off	and	walked	from it	In

er	Badstube	aber	hatten	sie	ein	rechtes	Höllenfeuer
e	bath room	however	had	they	a	true	hell fire

ngemacht,	daß	die	schöne	junge	Königin	bald	ersticken
rned on	that	the	beautiful	young	queen	soon	suffocate

1ußte.
id to
vould)

Is	das	vollbracht	war,	nahm	die	Alte	ihre	Tochter,
s	it	achieved	was	took	the	old one	her	daughter

etzte	ihr	eine	Haube	auf	und	legte	sie	ins	Bett	an
it	it	a	hood	on	and	put	it	in the	bed	in

er	Königin	Stelle.	Sie	gab	ihr	auch	die	Gestalt	und
e	queen's	place	She	gave	her	also	the	shape	and

as	Ansehen	der	Königin;	nur	das	verlorene	Auge
e	looks	of the	queen	only	the	lost	eye

onnte	sie	ihr	nicht	wiedergeben.	Damit	es	aber	der
'uld	she	her	not	give back	So that	it	however	the

önig	nicht	merkte,	mußte	sie	sich	auf	die	Seite
ng	not	noticed	had to	she	herself	on	the	side

'gen,	wo	sie	kein	Auge	hatte.
it	where	she	no	eye	had

Am	Abend,	als	er	heimkam	und	hörte,	daß	ihm	ein
In the	evening	as	he	came home	and	heard	that	to him	a

Söhnlein	geboren	war,	freute	er	sich	herzlich	und	wollte
little son	born	was	was pleased	he	himself	heartily	and	wanted

ans	Bett	seiner	lieben	Frau	gehen	und	sehen,	was
to the	bed	of his	beloved	wife	go	and	see	what (how)

sie	machte.	Da	rief	die	Alte	geschwind:	"Beileibe,	laßt
she	did	There	called	the	old one	quickly	By all means	leave

die	Vorhänge	zu,	die	Königin	darf	noch	nicht	ins	Licht
the	curtains	closed	the	queen	may	as of yet	not	in the	light

sehen	und	muß	Ruhe	haben."	Der	König	ging	zurück
see	and	must	rest	have	The	king	went	back

und	wußte	nicht,	daß	eine	falsche	Königin	im	Bette
and	knew	not	that	a	false	queen	in the	bed

lag.	Als	es	aber	Mitternacht	war	und	alles	schlief,	da
lay	As	it	however	midnight	was	and	everybody	slept	there

sah	die	Kinderfrau,	die	in	der	Kinderstube	neben	der
saw	the	nanny	who	in	the	children's room	beside	the

Wiege	saß	und	allein	noch	wachte,	wie	die	Tür
cradle	sat	and	alone	still	was awake	how	the	door

aufging	und	die	rechte	Königin	hereintrat.
opened	and	the	right , true	queen	stepped in

Sie	nahm	das	Kind	aus	der	Wiege,	legte	es	in	ihren
She	took	the	child	out of	the	cradle	put	it	on	her

Arm	und	gab	ihm	zu	trinken.	Dann	schüttelte	sie	ihm
arm	and	gave	it	to	drink	Then	shook up		she	him

sein	Kißchen,	legte	es	wieder	hinein.	Sie	vergaß	aber
his	pillow	put	it	again	back in	She	forgot	however

auch	das	Rehchen	nicht,	ging	in	die	Ecke,	wo	es
also	the	little deer	not	went	in	the	corner	where	it

lag,	und	streichelte	ihm	über	den	Rücken.
laid	and	stroked	it	over	the	back

Darauf	ging	sie	wieder	zur	Tür	hinaus,	und	die
Thereupon	went	she	again	to the	door	outside	and	the

Kinderfrau	fragte	am	andern	Morgen	die	Wächter,	ob
nanny	asked	on the	other (next)	morning	the	guards	whether

jemand	während	der	Nacht	ins	Schloß	gegangen	wäre,
someone	during	the	night	in the	castle	gone	had been

aber	sie	antworteten:
but	they	answered

"Nein,	wir	haben	niemand	gesehen."
No	we	have	nobody	seen

So   kam   sie   viele   Nächte und   sprach niemals   ein   Wort
So   came   she   many   nights and   spoke   never   one   word

dabei; die   Kinderfrau sah   sie   immer, aber   sie   getraute
thereby the   nanny   saw   her   always but   she   trusted
(during it)

sich   nicht, jemand   etwas   davon   zu   sagen.
herself   not   someone   something   of it   to   say

Als   nun   so   eine   Zeit   verflossen   war,   da   hub   die
As   now   so   a   while   passed   was   there , then   started   the
                                                                                (anheben; to begin)

Königin   in   der   Nacht   an   zu   reden   und   sprach:
queen   in   the   night   (on)   to   talk   and   spoke
                                    (anheben; to begin)

"Was   macht   mein   Kind?
What   makes   my   child
(How)   (does)

Was   macht   mein   Reh?
What   makes   my   deer
(How)   (does)

Nun   komm'   ich   noch   zweimal
Now   come   I   still   twice

Und   dann   nimmermehr."
and   then   never more

186 Brüder- Und Schwesterchen

Die	Kinderfrau	antwortete	ihr	nicht,	aber	als	sie	wieder
The	nanny	answered	her	not	but	as	it	again

verschwunden	war,	ging	sie	zum	König	und	erzählte
disappeared	was	went	she	to the	king	and	told

ihm	alles.	Sprach	der	König:	"Ach	Gott,	was	ist	das?
him	everything	Spoke	the	king	Oh	God	what	is	that

Ich	will	in	der	nächsten	Nacht	bei	dem	Kinde
I	shall	in	the	following	night	by	the	child

wachen."	Abends	ging	er	in	die	Kinderstube,	aber	um
wake	In the evening	went	he	in	the	child's room	but	at

Mitternacht	erschien	die	Königin	und	sprach:
midnight	appeared	the	queen	and	spoke

"Was	macht	mein	Kind?
What (How)	makes (does)	my	child

Was	macht	mein	Reh?
What (How)	makes (does)	my	deer

Nun	komm'	ich	noch	einmal
Now	come	I	still	once

Und	dann	nimmermehr."
And	then	never more

Und   sie   pflegte   dann   das   Kind,   wie   sie   gewöhnlich
And   she   cared for   then   the   child   as   she   usually

tat,   ehe   sie   verschwand.   Der   König   getraute   sich   nicht,
did   before   she   disappeared   The   king   trusted   himself   not

sie   anzureden,   aber   er   wachte   auch   in   der   folgenden
her   to address   but   he   waked   also   in   the   following

Nacht.   Sie   sprach   abermals:
night   She   spoke   again

"Was   macht   mein   Kind?
What   makes   my   child
(How)   (does)

Was   macht   mein   Reh?
What   makes   my   deer
(How)   (does)

Nun   komm'   ich   noch   diesmal
Now   come   I   still   this time

Und   dann   nimmermehr."
And   then   never more

Da   konnte   sich   der   König   nicht   zurückhalten,   sprang   zu
There , Thencould   himself   the   king   not   hold back   jumped   to

ihr   und   sprach: "Du   kannst   niemand   anders   sein   als
her   and   spoke   You   can   nobody   else   be   as
(but)

meine   liebe   Frau."
my   beloved   wife

Da antwortete sie: "Ja, ich bin deine liebe Frau", und
Then answered she Yes I am your dear wife and

hatte in dem Augenblick durch Gottes Gnade das
had in that moment through God's grace the

Leben wiedererhalten, war frisch, rot und gesund.
ife regained was fresh red and healthy

Darauf erzählte sie dem König den Frevel, den die
Whereupon told she the king the crime that the

böse Hexe und ihre Tochter an ihr verübt hatten. Der
evil witch and her daughter to her committed had The

König ließ beide vor Gericht führen, und es ward
king left both before court lead and it was

hnen das Urteil gesprochen. Die Tochter ward in den
hem the judgement spoken The daughter was in the

Wald geführt, wo sie die wilden Tiere zerrissen, die
orest led where her the wild animals tore up the

Hexe aber ward ins Feuer gelegt und mußte
witch however was in the fire put and had to

ammervoll verbrennen.
miserably burn

Und wie sie zu Asche verbrannt war, verwandelte sich
And as she to ashes burned was transformed itself

das Rehkälbchen und erhielt seine menschliche Gestalt
the little deer calf and received its human shape

wieder; Schwesterchen und Brüderchen aber lebten
again little sister and little brother however lived

glücklich zusammen bis an ihr Ende.
happy together onto their end

The book you're now reading contains the paper or digital paper version of the powerful e-book application from Bermuda Word. Our software integrated e-books allow you to become fluent in German reading and listening, fast and easy! Go to learn-to-read-foreign-languages.com, and get the App version of this e-book!

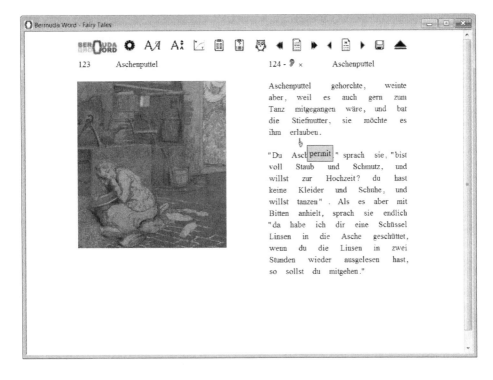

The standalone e-reader software contains the e-book text, includes audio and integrates **spaced repetition word practice** for **optimal language learning**. Choose your font type or size and read as you would with a regular e-reader. Stay immersed with **interlinear** or **immediate mouse-over pop-up translation** and click on difficult words to **add them to your wordlist**. The software knows which words are low frequency and need more practice.

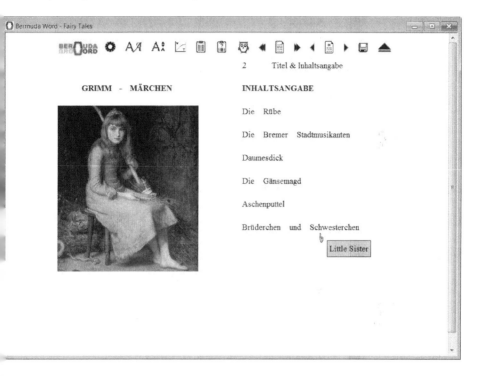

With the Bermuda Word e-book program you **memorize all words** fast and easy just by reading and listening and efficient practice!

LEARN-TO-READ-FOREIGN-LANGUAGES.COM
Contact us using the button on the site!